APHRA BEHN

THE ROVER

edited by Robyn Bolam

Professor of Literature at St Mary's College,
Strawberry Hill: a College of the University of Surrey

A & C Black • London
W W Norton • New York

First published 1995
Reprinted 2000, 2002, 2005, 2007
A & C Black Publishers Limited
38 Soho Square, London W1D 3HB
www.acblack.com

ISBN 978-0-7136-6671-7

A CIP catalogue for this book is available
from the British Library

This book is produced using paper made from wood grown in
managed, sustainable forests. It is natural, renewable and recyclable.
The logging and manufacturing processes conform to the environmental
regulations of the country of origin.

Printed in the UK by CPI Bookmarque, Croydon, CR0 4TD

CONTENTS

ACKNOWLEDGEMENTS

I owe a debt to all past and present editors of *The Rover*, particularly to Frederick M. Link (Regents Restoration Drama Series; Lincoln, Nebr., and London, 1967) and Janet Todd (*Oroonoko, The Rover and Other Works*, London, 1992). Bill Naismith's reprint of Montague Summers' edition (London, 1993 and 1915 respectively) and Maureen Duffy's collection *Five Plays* (London, 1990) were also consulted. Many of the texts listed in 'Further Reading' proved invaluable. I would like to thank the staff of the British Library, Ms Anne Watts, and Dr Marion O'Connor for their assistance, and I am extremely grateful to Professor Brian Gibbons for his help and guidance throughout the preparation of this volume.

ABBREVIATIONS

B.L.	British Library
C	First collected edition, 1702
C2	Collected edition, 1724
It.	Italian
LTW	*The London Theatre World: 1660–1800*, ed. Robert D. Hume, Carbondale and Edwardsville, 1980
OED	*The Oxford English Dictionary*
om.	omitted
Q1	First Quarto, 1677
Q2	Second Quarto, 1697
Q3	Third Quarto, 1709
S	*The Works of Aphra Behn*, ed. Montague Summers, vol. 1, London, 1915
s.d.	stage direction
s.p.	speech prefix
T	*Oroonoko, The Rover and Other Works*, ed. Janet Todd, London, 1992

INTRODUCTION

THE AUTHOR

THE MOST persuasive evidence suggests that Aphra Behn was born in 1640,[1] a year of political crisis during which Charles I's eleven years of personal rule ended, the theatres were closed, and the country moved rapidly towards civil war. She would therefore have been nine when the king was beheaded at Whitehall and grew up through the years of the Commonwealth, appropriately coming of age just after the Restoration of Charles II in 1660 and the reopening of the theatres. Her adult life coincided with the reigns of Charles and his brother, who became James II: she died on 16 April 1689,[2] two months into the reign of William III and James's daughter, Mary.

We still do not have a complete picture of Behn's life: the few recorded details are sometimes contradictory and errors have caused further confusion.[3] The most likely candidates for her parents are Bartholomew Johnson, a barber of Canterbury in Kent, and his wife, Elizabeth (née Denham): an Aphra Johnson was baptised at Harbledown, near Canterbury, on 14 December 1640. Anne, Countess of Winchilsea, referred to Behn in her poem 'The Circuit of Apollo', and commented in a note:

> Mrs Behn was Daughter to a Barber, who liv'd formerly in Wye, a little market Town (now much decay'd) in Kent: though the account of her life before her Works pretends otherwise; some persons now alive do testify upon their knowledge that to be her Original.[4]

---

[1] Most critics now agree, although Sara Heller Mendelson argues for a date at the end of the 1640s (*The Mental World of Stuart Women*, Brighton, 1987, p. 116) and Janet Todd also raises the possibility of a date after 1640 (T, p. 2).

[2] *The Life and Memoirs ... by One of the Fair Sex*, in Aphra Behn, *The Histories and Novels of the Late Ingenious Mrs Behn*, London, 1696 (B.L. Catalogue no. C.57.K.24) gives 1686 as the date of Behn's death. Thomas Culpepper (Colepeper) agrees on 1689 in his *Adversaria* (B.L. Harley MS 7588, p. 426 v. and p. 453 v.), but differs on the day, giving 16 and 29 April respectively.

[3] In *The Dictionary of National Biography*, Edmund Gosse lists an Aphra Johnson, baptised on 10 July 1640. This has since been shown to be an Aphra Amis, who was buried two days later. See Jane Jones, 'New light on the background and early life of Aphra Behn' in *Notes and Queries* 235 (1990), 289.

[4] *The Poems of Anne Countess of Winchilsea: from the original ed. of 1713 and from unpublished ms*, ed. M. Reynolds (Decennial Publications Series 2, vol. 5), Chicago, 1903, p. 427; B.L. Catalogue no. AC2691d/11

Behn's knowledge of languages and her writing ability suggested to many biographers that she had received an education and must, therefore, have been of a higher social station than the daughter of a barber. As Anne, Countess of Winchilsea, infers, perhaps even the first biographical piece, *The Life and Memoirs ... by One of the Fair Sex*, published in 1696 and written not long after Behn's death as a preface to her collected fictional works, made such an assumption.[5] The note to 'The Circuit of Apollo' has been described as 'dubious Kentish gossip', or maliciousness on the part of the countess, but Jane Jones points out that the information accords with a number of contemporary documents relating to Bartholomew Johnson and that Anne, Countess of Winchilsea, lived in the area and might be expected to know that Aphra Behn was not, as *The Life and Memoirs* stated, 'a gentlewoman by birth'.

Yet Behn was no ordinary barber's daughter. On her mother's side she appears to have had higher social connections, despite Elizabeth Denham's inability or disinclination to sign her name on her marriage allegation in 1638.[6] Behn's parents married, apparently, to legalise the status of their first child, Frances, who had already been conceived – but if, as Jane Jones believes, Elizabeth Denham had a brother, George, who attended university and eventually became a doctor,[7] Aphra's mother may have traded the higher social status available to her by birth for a more humble, married respectability. She also found employment as a wet nurse to a gentle family. In Thomas Culpepper's *Adversaria*, probably written shortly after Behn's death, it is noted that:

> Her mother was the Colonell Culpeppers nurse & gave him suck for some time. Mrs Been was born at Sturrey or Canterbury, her name was Johnson, so that she might be called Ben Johnson, she had also a fayer sister maryed to Capt. Write, their Names were ffranck, & Aphora, was Mr. Beene.[8]

Earlier in the manuscript Behn is called 'foster sister to the Colonell, her mother being the Colonell's nurse' and described as 'a most beautiful woman and a most excellent poet'. It is now assumed that the writer was Sir Thomas Culpepper, an orphan from the age of five, and that he and 'the Colonell' were the same person. The description of Aphra Behn as a 'foster sister' to Sir Thomas might be no more than an expression of their

[5] See note 2 above.
[6] Canterbury Cathedral Library, uncatalogued
[7] See Jones, 'New light', 290.
[8] See note 2 above. Culpepper was born in 1637 and the Johnsons' first child was baptised on 6 December 1638, so it is conceivable that Elizabeth Johnson was his wet nurse for a time.

closeness as children: his affection for and admiration of her is apparent. If she was treated as one of the family she would also have enjoyed certain privileges not usually accorded to a barber's daughter, and these provide a possible explanation for her education. Living in Canterbury, *en route* to the continent, Behn would also have had daily opportunities to hear several European languages: Jones notes the abundance of 'French-speaking Huguenot refugees' in the city and the 'large Dutch Congregation' in 'nearby Sandwich'.[9]

In 1663, at the age of 23, Behn travelled with her family on the appointment of her father as Lieutenant-General of the English colony of Surinam and thirty-six other islands. Jones suggests that this unlikely occurrence may have been a result of Bartholomew Johnson and his daughter's involvement in pro-Royalist activities during the 1659 attempt to restore the king,[10] but no evidence for this has been found. Behn's father apparently died on the journey and, after approximately two months in Surinam, the family left. Not long afterwards Aphra Johnson became Aphra Behn. She may have married a London merchant of 'Dutch extraction', as the *Life and Memoirs* states, or the German ('ffranck') Johan Behn, who sailed in the West Indies, possibly on the boat which brought the Johnsons back from Surinam, as Jones plausibly argues – or it might be that, as a prelude to earning an independent living in the theatre, Aphra looked for inspiration to a great dramatist who died three years before she was born – adding the 'h' in her maiden name to his forename, and wittily making herself 'Behn Johnson'.[11]

No marriage records for Behn exist and she never refers to a husband: the man most documented in her life was John Hoyle, a bisexual lawyer. Whether she experienced an arranged marriage with an elderly man who died of plague shortly after, whether she married a younger able seaman on impulse and quickly separated, or whether she remained unmarried throughout her life is still unproven. We do know that Thomas Killigrew recruited her to spy for Charles II in the Dutch wars of 1666, but she was not paid for her trouble and was threatened with, if not actually subjected to, incarceration in a debtors' prison in 1668, her pleas to Killigrew and the king apparently having been ignored. Perhaps as a result of this treatment, although she had

[9] See Jones, 'New light', 291.

[10] Ibid., 292

[11] Thomas Culpepper remarked on the combination of names and Mary Ann O'Donnell also makes this suggestion ('Tory wit and unconventional woman: Aphra Behn' in *Women Writers of the Seventeenth Century*, ed. Katharina M. Wilson and Frank J. Warnke, Athens, Ga., 1989, p. 352).

presented an Indian costume to Killigrew's King's Company on her return from Surinam, her plays were performed by the rival Duke's Company from 1670. Between 1670 and 1689 she produced eighteen plays, being the most prolific playwright of her day, second only to Dryden. Frances Boothby, Margaret Cavendish, Katherine Philips, and Elizabeth Polwhele were all contemporary women fellow-playwrights, but Aphra Behn was the first female professional writer in England, and was greatly acclaimed. She was an inspiration for budding writers, both male and female; a poet and editor of miscellanies; a pioneer of the short novel – her most famous being *Oroonoko* (1688), an abolitionary work – a writer of short stories; and a translator of texts in several languages. Subject to literary misogyny, slandered as well as praised in her own time and since, Behn's work is only now being appreciated as it deserves.

Although her family may have been Protestant (her father was made Overseer of the Poor for St Margaret's Parish in Canterbury in 1654),[12] there are several indications that, at the end of her life at least, Aphra Behn was a Catholic;[13] yet, in the new Protestant reign, she was given the rare privilege of burial in the cloisters of Westminster Abbey on 20 April 1689. Her black marble slab is inscribed:

> Here lies a proof that wit can never be
> Defence enough against mortality.[14]

Perhaps not; but the wit of the woman known as Astrea has proved an admirable defence against many other things, ensuring her continued popularity.

DATE AND SOURCES

The Rover was first performed and the play text published in 1677. Copies of three issues of the first Quarto still exist; they exhibit minor differences, mainly in their title-pages and post-scripts. The licensing date is given as 2 July 1677. Although she was the acknowledged author of at least four plays by the time she wrote *The Rover*, Aphra Behn or her publisher chose to bring out its first issue and most of its second anonymously. Only towards the end of the second issue's printing run was the phrase 'especially of our sex' inserted after 'dominion' at line 23 of the postscript – a hint that she was no longer attempting to conceal

---

[12] Canterbury Cathedral Library J/Q/453i. See Jones, 'New light', 293.
[13] See Gerald Duchovnay, 'Aphra Behn's religion', *Notes and Queries* 221 (1976), 235–7.
[14] Reproduced in Thomas Culpepper's *Adversaria*, p. 426 r.

her identity – and the title-page of the third issue printed the author's name: Mrs A. Behn.

The postscript, only printed in the first Quarto, acknowledges occasional similarities with Richard Brome's *The Novella* (1632); Frederick Link identifies these as hints for I.ii.336–50, the balcony scene in II.i with Angellica's suitors, and suggestions for Florinda's letter to Belvile in I.ii.[15] *The Novella* may also be seen to contain an early version of Angellica Bianca. However, Aphra Behn's main source for *The Rover* was a lengthy closet drama by Thomas Killigrew, *Thomaso, or The Wanderer*, which was written in 1654.[16] Behn borrowed substantially from Killigrew, and the opening of her postscript suggests that this was probably the reason why *The Rover* did not bear its author's name from the outset as, following 'a report about town . . . that [*The Rover* was] *Thomaso* altered . . . the booksellers fear some trouble from the proprietor of that admirable play'.

Before she wrote *The Rover*, Aphra Behn transformed and improved a number of plays by dramatists such as George Wilkins and Brome, but it was not usual for her to appropriate large sections of dialogue word for word, as she did from *Thomaso*. Even in this case she was not a plagiarist in the usual sense: her relationship with her source material becomes clearer if we focus on her innovations and changes, rather than on basic similarities such as a plot based on the adventures of banished cavaliers, and her use of existing dramatic figures who provided the foundations for a whole range of characters from Willmore, Florinda, Blunt, and Angellica Bianca to Don Pedro, Antonio, Callis, Lucetta, Sancho, and Philippo. When she retained the names of Killigrew's characters, as in the case of Angellica Bianca, Behn often altered their personalities and actions so that they are presented as new creations, and Killigrew's dialogue may occasionally be reproduced (e.g. at I.i.129–34), but when assigned to a new character (particularly one of a different sex) and rearranged, the force of its impact is increased.

She was adept at creating moments of dramatic tension and, by condensing, cutting, refocusing, and making important additions to Killigrew's text, she quickened its pace considerably and made it into a successful and performable drama.[17] Some

---

[15] Frederick M. Link, ed., *The Rover* (Regents Restoration Drama Series), Lincoln, Nebr., and London, 1967, p. 130

[16] *Thomaso* was printed in London in 1663 in Killigrew's *Comedies and Tragedies* (B.L. Catalogue no. C.39.K.4).

[17] See also J. De Ritter, 'The gypsy, the rover, and the wanderer: Aphra Behn's revision of Thomas Killigrew', *Restoration: Studies in English Literary Culture 1660–1700* 10 (1986), 82–92.

differences are major: Behn invented Valeria and paired her with Frederick to form another couple; she split Killigrew's Thomaso into two – his wanderer element lives on in Willmore, the rover, while his faithful qualities are developed in a new character, Belvile. Hellena is Behn's invention although, surprisingly, she borrowed from Killigrew's Harrigo ('a sober English gentleman') and even from *Thomaso*'s so-called 'good courtesans', Angellica and Paulina, for some of her speeches and, in the case of the latter, part of her background. Blunt, who is closely based on Killigrew's Edwardo, came to life when Behn redefined his role in relation to the main plot and, by associating him with the catch-phrase ''adsheartlikins', gave him a character we do not forget.

While Killigrew modelled Thomaso on himself, as the name suggests, Behn most probably incorporated elements of John Wilmot, Earl of Rochester, into Willmore. She knew Rochester, as did the famous actress Elizabeth Barry, who initially played the part of Hellena. In portraying the allure of a character of such self-professed, though single-sexed promiscuity, she may also have been drawing on her own relationship with John Hoyle. The most famous rover of them all was, of course, Charles II, who, according to 'Tory mythology ... on the verge of fleeing England, disguised himself in buff'[18] – so not only Willmore's libertinism but even his costume is linked to the 'Prince' he serves in the play.

Although she cut Angellica Bianca's involvement in the action, Behn strengthened both character and plot by doing so. Killigrew's Angellica regards herself as a victim and remains in love with Thomaso at the close: she is not allowed to control her fate, being ignorant of the arrangement by which Thomaso and Don Pedro agree to dispose of her. Behn's character is more forceful, refuses to see herself as being morally inferior, and attempts to make her own decisions. Behn also gave her the power to hold Willmore at pistol-point, finally sparing his life. Killigrew created characters through whom he advocated female emancipation (such as Harrigo), but Behn tackled the issue in a much more thorough manner. Above all, the biggest difference in these two plays is one of liveliness of atmosphere, rather than specific characters or instances: Behn produced a drama in which the spirit of carnival is paramount.

[18] Susan Staves, *Players' Scepters: Fictions of Authority in the Restoration*, Lincoln, Nebr., 1979, p. 2

'THE ROVER' AND CARNIVAL

Killigrew's *Thomaso*, on which *The Rover* was based, is set in Madrid in late November. There are disguises, and the Feast of St Cecilia, patron saint of music, is associated with Thomaso himself, but there is none of the pre-Lenten urgency to eat, drink, and be merry which characterises *The Rover*, and no mention of the pervading spirit of carnival which Aphra Behn introduced when she adapted and altered Killigrew's play. Behn also moved the action to Naples, where a carnival setting was associated with Roman Saturnalian revels as well as with opposition to the restrictions of the Christian tradition's Lent, which included a ban on sexual intercourse as well as the eating of meat.

If a festive spirit seems restrained in *Thomaso* this is hardly surprising. Killigrew's text was reputedly written in exile in 1654. At home, Cromwell had dissolved the Rump Parliament and set himself up as Lord Protector. It was a time of disputes and foreign wars; Royalist plots were being revived to displace Cromwell, who seemed to be taking the country back to a monarchy with himself as king. *Thomaso* was a closet drama which could not be performed at the time of writing because the theatres were closed and, even if this had not been the case, a play of its nature would have been forbidden. It was printed in 1663, after the Restoration of Charles II, when the cavaliers it celebrated were comfortably returned home – but there is no evidence that it was ever acted.

When Behn produced *The Rover* the monarchy had been re-established for seventeen years. Mikhail Bakhtin has observed that 'Moments of death and revival, of change and renewal always led to a festive perception of the world'[19] – but neither renewal nor change could be said to be being celebrated in 1677. If it was not pure nostalgia, on what was Aphra Behn's use of carnival based?

The play's period setting in the 1650s is very significant. Cromwell's Protectorate had suppressed pastimes and sports and, to Royalists, the period must have seemed like an indefinite extension of Lent. Joining in the festivities of carnival which were denied them at home, exiled cavaliers whiled away the time until the new order of the once-revolutionary Parliamentarians could be overthrown. Instead of being a wealthy, extravagant elite, the exiles had lost lands and money: they were now displaced and marginalised in foreign parts, and Behn's play continually

---

[19] Mikhail Bakhtin, *Rabelais and His World*, trans. Helene Iswolsky, Bloomington, Ind., 1984, p. 9

stresses their 'outsider' status. Willmore is not just a rover – a pirate, one who wanders, an inconstant lover – he is a 'Tramontana rover' (V.i.400), which, apart from signifying someone uncouth, indicates a foreigner or stranger. In fact, most of the characters are outsiders of one kind or another: Naples is under Spanish rule, Angellica Bianca is introduced as a native of Padua, even the English are divided into the impecunious cosmopolitan cavaliers and the wealthy traveller from the country, whom they befriend but constantly taunt because he never committed himself politically and kept his privileges and estate. Established incomers prey upon more recent arrivals: Lucetta exploits Blunt's ignorance of Naples and of her ways – though she does worry that her treatment of him may put paid to future dealings with foreigners if word gets around (III.iii.49–51). The protagonists, then, are all away from their home ground and are vulnerable because of this. The usual social hierarchies are inverted. The Spanish, old enemies of the English, are either in power officially (Don Antonio is the viceroy's son) or unofficially (Philippo takes the spoils Lucetta tricks from Blunt and reminds us of the old quarrel about the Spanish Armada in his reference to 'old Queen Bess's' gold and the 'quarrel . . . since eighty-eight' (III.iii.44–5). The English, who might have been gentlemen at home, are poor, riotous, and often despised abroad.

Although the victimisation of prostitutes was a common feature of traditional carnival, Behn does not condemn either Lucetta or Angellica Bianca but rather, at significant moments, gives them the upper hand over the English strangers, an even more disadvantaged and male social group. No matter how brave they may be, abroad they are distinguished principally by their lack of riches and often run-down appearance; even a courtesan's servant feels free to mock Willmore in his presence with 'I believe those breeches and he have been acquainted ever since he was beaten at Worcester' (II.ii.22–4). Blunt has managed to retain his wealth, being no cavalier, yet he does not have the wit to keep it and escape abuse. Lucetta soon picks him out as a gullible fool:

> He's English too, and they say that's a sort of good-natured loving people, and have generally so kind an opinion of themselves that a woman with any wit may flatter 'em into any sort of fool she pleases.   (I.ii.220–3)

This is gender specific, unlike the jibe in *Hamlet* that the English are all mad: Behn's joke implies that, at home and abroad, an English male is no match for any woman's wit. Both Lucetta and Angellica are victims of a male- centred society and an economy which treats them as a commodity, but each has her own methods of survival built on compromise, and they manipulate the men on whom they depend. The 'jilting wench', Lucetta, gains great wealth without giving any favours to a country gentleman, while the 'famous courtesan', who demands a ridiculously high price, eventually chooses to bestow herself for nothing on a penniless pirate and, when she cannot command his constant love, holds him at pistol-point to revenge her honour. Angellica may not win Willmore, yet she retains his admiration and the adoration and respect of someone as rich and powerful as the viceroy's son.

Behn's women are more certain of their intrinsic worth than Killigrew's female characters. They reserve the right to adjust their monetary price as it suits them, being more financially secure than many of the men in the play. Even the upright Belvile is dependent on marrying into money (the box of jewels which Florinda, his Spanish love, hides in the garden may be a metaphor for the virtue she has so much difficulty preserving, but since Jessica's flight to Lorenzo in Shakespeare's *The Merchant of Venice*, it is also a symbol of the defiant woman who breaks through family and cultural opposition to give herself and her wealth to the man of her choice). The woman-shy Frederick also has his future determined by Florinda, who tells him:

> I'll be reconciled to you on one condition – that you'll follow the example of your friend in marrying a maid that does not hate you, and whose fortune (I believe) will not be unwelcome to you.   (V.i.172–5)

This world, where women can take the initiative, is the world of carnival. It is a time of misrule; everything is turned upside down, prohibitions are temporarily removed, and privileges and rank suspended. Everyone, however different, can be integrated by joining in. As Bakhtin wrote:

> Carnival is not a spectacle seen by the people; they live in it, and everyone participates because its very idea embraces all the people. While carnival lasts, there is no other life outside it. During carnival time life is subject only to its laws, that is, the laws of its own freedom.[20]

Carnival may have appealed to Restoration audiences because of its emphasis on sexual freedom, and to Aphra Behn because it extended this freedom to women as well as men. Male dramatists also created outspoken and daring women characters. Etherege's *The Man of Mode*, which was performed the year before *The Rover*, is part of a movement discernible in Restoration comedy away from a focus on the male lead and towards an awareness that 'his lady', in this case Harriet Woodvil, was the real 'centre of interest'.[21] The fact that women were now playing

[20] Ibid., p. 7
[21] Donald Bruce, *Topics of Restoration Comedy*, New York, 1974, p. 135

women's parts, coupled with Behn's influence in the contemporary theatre, probably helped to bring about this transition.
Certainly one topic which was close to Behn's heart was the issue
of arranged marriages and a woman's right to choose her own
husband: beginning with her first play, *The Forced Marriage*, she
tackled the topic at least eleven times in her dramatic works.

Unlike *Thomaso*, *The Rover* does not begin by focusing on the
men: it opens with Hellena and Florinda discussing their lack
of independence. Both women display the confidence to have
opinions and desires – and to express them. Only Lucetta, of all
the females in the play, seems unable to do this – perhaps because
she merely exploits the carnival spirit for financial gain at the
command of Philippo and is always under his control. She never
manages to break free and act as she would wish. As she tells
him, speaking of Blunt: 'And art thou not an unmerciful rogue,
not to afford him one night for all this? I should not have been
such a Jew' (III.iii.59–61). But she is not allowed to follow her
own desires because, as Philippo reminds her, he wants 'to keep
as much of thee as I can to myself'. Lucetta, like Angellica,
demonstrates how difficult it is for women – especially kept
women and prostitutes – to retain their sexual freedom. Dependent on men financially for their survival, they cannot afford the
luxury of dispensing favours at will. Angellica, with her greater
independence and wealth, fares better than Lucetta. She also,
like Hellena and Florinda, has the advantage of a female ally.
Her woman, Moretta, is probably motivated more by economic
considerations than emotional attachment, but we feel sure that
when Angellica finally turns her back on Willmore, Moretta will
be there to help her return to her old, confident state. Similarly,
in I.i Hellena fiercely takes her sister's part in criticising their
father's wishes and her brother's intentions to carry them out;
later, Valeria rushes to the rescue when Hellena and Florinda
find themselves under threat. Supportive, energetic women are
Behn's speciality.

Behn has been credited with creating more daring dialogue
between the sexes than many of her male contemporaries. In *The
Rover* this could be due in part to her use of Killigrew's text
(which is freer than most in this respect) and particularly to her
reassignment to Hellena of certain speeches which Killigrew
allocated to a male character – but the freedom with which her
men and women converse is also due to the way in which another
aspect of carnival is allowed to flourish. Hellena has already
entered fully into its spirit when the play opens, 'Nay, I'm
resolved to provide myself this carnival, if there be e'er a handsome proper fellow of my humour above ground, though I ask
first' (I.i.40–3). She has resolved to find her own man and initiate

a relationship: her father and brother may be planning to save the cost of a dowry by placing her in a convent, but she is quite aware of what she has to offer – and to gain by making other plans. Her sister, Florinda, has already determined to defy their father and refuses to marry 'the rich old Don Vincentio', being equally sure of her worth: 'I shall let him see I understand better what's due to my beauty, birth, and fortune, and more – to my soul, than to obey those unjust commands' (I.i.24–7).

Both are set for battle when their brother, Don Pedro, enters. He apparently does not notice Hellena at first and addresses only Florinda, which suggests that he believes Hellena, the novice, to be elsewhere praying – an impression reinforced by his surprise when she cannot resist butting into the conversation to take Florinda's part. Hellena not only disobeys his command to 'Go – up to your devotion' (he leaves before she does), but she fiercely challenges everything he says, mocks Vincentio's lack of virility, and shocks Pedro with her tenacity ('Have you done yet?') and her outspoken language. Behn toned down Killigrew's description of the old prospective husband who 'farts as loud as a Musket for a jest' to 'sighs a belch or two, loud as a musket', but reserved the detail for greater impact later in Hellena's outraged, 'What then? The viceroy's son is better than that old Sir Fisty'. Pedro, shocked by his sister's disrespectful term ('old fart')[22] for her father's choice of husband, orders her immediate incarceration for the duration of the carnival, followed at Lent by 'her everlasting penance in a monastery'.

For Hellena, the carnival has already begun: she is indulging in vigorous colloquial outspokenness – her free expression of oaths ('Now hang me if . . .' I.i.28) and her skills of witty mockery make her a natural sparring partner for the outspoken Willmore. Hellena looks to the carnival to provide her with experience of love and life and, as Elin Diamond aptly expresses it, 'She exercises her will only by pursuing and winning Willmore, for as it turns out he has the "more" she "would fain know" '.[23] Unlike Lent, carnival is characterised by abundance and easy gratification. Willmore steps ashore in search of 'Love and mirth' in a 'warm climate' after having been deprived of women and good living on board ship. He may stink 'of tar and ropes' ends like a dock or pesthouse' (I.ii.102) but he has an abundance of persuasive rhetoric as well as desire: 'I have a world of love in store.

---

[22] See textual note to I.i.143. This is not the only reading, but it is plausible – and less tautological than the alternative.

[23] Elin Diamond, 'Gestus and signature in Aphra Behn's *The Rover*', *ELH* 56 (1989), 528. See also David M. Sullivan, 'The female will in Aphra Behn', *Women's Studies* 22 (1993), 335–47.

Would you would ... take some on't off my hands' (I.ii.164–6). While he has been confined to male company at sea, Hellena has been pent up in a nunnery and, like him, she is eager to start making up for lost time: 'for when I begin, I fancy I shall love like anything; I never tried yet' (I.ii.205–6). She has no intention of dying 'a maid, and in a captain's hands too' (V.i.438–9), but the liberality of carnival does not mean that she has forgotten the realities of everyday life. Hellena's gipsy disguise *is* only a disguise: she does not really want a life of hardship and 'A cradle full of noise and mischief, with a pack of repentance at my back' (V.i.473–5). Her plain speaking and scorn of Willmore's attempts to win her persuade him into a marriage 'bargain' which, although both enter defensively, she has engineered. Perhaps marriage is as unattractive to her as it is to Willmore but, without it, the freedom to explore her sexual desires could take her back to the convent as an abandoned, unmarriageable young woman, with or without a child. Marriage may have its faults but a nunnery has few pleasures for a woman of her nature.

When Hellena first hears about Florinda's love for Belvile, she declares, 'I hope he has some mad companion or other that will spoil my devotion' (I.i.39–40), and from that point on she exerts all her energies to provoke an assault on her virginity, advertising it at every opportunity, confident that she has the wit to handle the situation to her ultimate advantage. Florinda, on the other hand, is constantly fending off attempted rape from the time of her first meeting with Belvile, 'when I was exposed to such dangers as the licensed lust of common soldiers threatened when rage and conquest flew through the city' (I.i.79–82). The Englishmen like to think they are no common soldiers intent on rape and pillage, but in Willmore's drunken assault on Florinda in III.v and the mass rape planned in Act IV by Blunt with the compliance, at one point, of Frederick and the others, a modern audience may begin to doubt. While indecent behaviour towards women is part of the carnival tradition and Restoration drama frequently incorporates a physical assault on a virtuous heroine (even Nahum Tate's rewriting of *King Lear* includes an attempted rape of Cordelia), Aphra Behn's treatment of the issue raises far-reaching questions concerning sexual violence against women (particularly of different social stations) and the problems involved in the way female chastity was prized, protected, and put under siege.

The Rover's carnival setting highlights the double standards normally practised by both men and women. A society in which rich old men take young wives they cannot satisfy encourages the latter to 'ramble to supply the defects of some grave impotent husband' (IV.v.82–3) and allows women like Lucetta to use this as a cover for deception and robbery. When, as Belvile insists, there are wealthy 'whores' who do not fit the traditional stereotype, and wealthy wives doing much the same but without the fee, how is a man like Blunt to discern whether he is predator or prey?

> Why yes, sir, they are whores, though they'll neither entertain you with drinking, swearing, or bawdry; are whores in all those gay clothes and right jewels ... with those great houses richly furnished ... are whores, and arrant ones. (II.i.77–82)

The men perpetuate a situation where the honour of their own women is valued and fiercely defended, but a woman without an effective protector is seen as fair game or, as Willmore puts it, 'another prize' (III.i.320). When circumstances temporarily remove a woman from family or marital protection, the men become victims of each other's prejudices and lusts. For all his boasting, Frederick has little experience of women; he acts according to the primitive distinctions that governed much male behaviour at the time, 'I begin to suspect something; and 'twould anger us vilely to be trussed up for a rape upon a maid of quality, when we only believe we ruffle a harlot' (IV.v.141–3). The 'harlot' is, of course, Florinda: Frederick's description of her earlier as 'that damned virtuous woman' (I.ii.20) is almost realised.

The farce, which provokes both laughter and unease as the masked Florinda is physically threatened by one male after another, reaches its climax when her own brother, who has been the fiercest defender of her honour, draws the longest sword in the contest to take possession of her body. Belvile is helpless, and only the timely intervention of Valeria saves the day. The ridiculous situation was brought about by Don Pedro's insistence that Florinda should marry the man of his choosing rather than her own, and that Hellena should be denied marriage altogether. Finally, Florinda's match is a *fait accompli*, and the strain of making a stand against that of Willmore and Hellena is too great. Don Pedro consents in the face of mass resistance, relieved to 'be free from fears of her honour'. 'Guard it you now, if you can', he tells Willmore, 'I have been a slave to't long enough' (V.i.552–3). Willmore's advice that 'a woman's honour is not worth guarding when she has a mind to part with it' (V.i.554–6) could be said to be the message of the play.

One freedom of carnival is the opportunity to act foolishly without regard to social position. In not opposing his sisters' marriages, Don Pedro bows to the prevailing pressures of festivity. It is a huge relief for him to relinquish the burden of patriarchal responsibility. Wickedly, Behn allows him to relish his liberation. When we first meet Pedro he is about to put on his masked costume and participate in revels he has forbidden to his sisters. By the end, in forgiving everyone, he has entered into the spirit of equality which characterises carnival life. One by one, male and female alike, the characters venture out: Florinda and Belvile to find each other, Hellena and Valeria to woo husbands, Pedro and Antonio to win Angellica, Blunt to seek an inexpensive woman, and Willmore to take any woman. Those who achieve their desires do so by complicated routes, often involving potential humiliation and risk: others are exposed to ridicule, danger, and defeat. Antonio is wounded, and Belvile, a victim of mistaken identity, is driven to participate in the equivalent of a carnivalesque mock duel. All are free to play the fool for a time, but if any person could be considered to have been elected King of Fools by his companions, that person must be Blunt.

He is victimised by Lucetta, Philippo, and Sancho in additional ways to those found in Killigrew's text, where his counterpart, Edwardo, is merely turned out of doors in his drawers in the night and is lost in the city streets by the equivalent of Sancho. Bakhtin notes that carnival hell included, amongst other things, a trap to catch fools, and Behn adds a Rabelaisian touch to Blunt's debasement by dropping him literally into excrement. On one level the foolish country fop becomes a hero of folk humour when he falls down the trapdoor into the sewer and undergoes a mock journey to the underworld, returning in the tradition of such folk heroes, to tell of the horrors he found there. At another level Blunt's fate can be seen as a veiled political comment. It is wished on him in I.ii by Frederick when, having noticed Blunt's disappearance in pursuit of Lucetta, he declares,

> I hope 'tis some common crafty sinner, one that will fit him. It may be she'll sell him for Peru: the rogue's sturdy, and would work well in a mine. At least I hope she'll dress him for our mirth, cheat him of all, then have him well-favouredly banged, and turned out naked at midnight.
>
> (I.ii.296–301)

The reason for Frederick's uncharacteristic vindictiveness becomes clear when Belvile catalogues details of Blunt's privileged upbringing. Never having known hardship or the sordid side of life, never having committed himself to a cause as they have done, and, therefore, never having risked life, limb, or fortune, the wealthy 'Essex calf' is a cause of deep-seated resentment – though this is usually overridden by good humour. It is as if the spirit of carnival allows Frederick's idle wish to be granted. Blunt is not sold to labour in a Peruvian mine, but he is forced underground and exposed to other nightmare experiences. He is also subjected to the carnivalesque removal of his fine clothes and their replacement with a clown-like costume – his underwear and 'an old rusty sword and buff belt'. His horrified response, 'Now, how like a morris dancer I am equipped!' (IV.v.8–9), and his equally disgusted view of himself in the Spanish habit he is forced to wear later signify his humiliation. Belvile's pronouncement on the new costume is telling: 'Methinks 'tis well, and makes thee look e'en cavalier' (V.i.579). Finally, even the Englishmen are equal – Blunt, with his possible parliamentarian leanings and fastidious fussing about his clothes, has at last to make do like one of the cavaliers.

In carnival time costume is crucial, and from the first scene of *The Rover* characters are changing their clothes and exchanging identities for a variety of purposes. When characters lose control of their state of dress, as in the case of Blunt and, later, of Florinda, who escapes to the garden 'in an undress' (III.v), their vulnerability is apparent. Hellena, however, always appears to have the situation in hand and makes successful transitions from novice's garb to gipsy costume, and finally to the boy's clothes she is wearing when Willmore agrees to marry her. Female cross-dressing was popular on the Restoration stage as a means of allowing the audience to view more of the woman playing the part, so Behn may have merely been catering to audience expectations here, but Willmore's possible associations with the Earl of Rochester and John Hoyle, both of whom pursued men as well as women, probably gave her choice an additional *frisson*. Historically, there is also a link between women who adopted male attire and certain prostitutes who used such dress to signal their profession. There is no indication that Hellena's appearance would have been viewed in this way, but the ambiguous natures of costume and masquerade in the play reveal the dangers of judging by appearances.

In I.ii Belvile explains to Blunt that the 'fine pretty creatures' he is admiring 'are, or would have you think they're courtesans, who … are to be hired by the month' (I.ii.89–90). By drawing attention in the drama to a confusion that extended from carnival into life beyond the play, Behn makes her audience question notions of respectability and notoriety in relation to women's sexuality. Nancy Copeland sees Behn's juxtapositioning of Hellena and Angellica resulting 'in a narrowing of the distance between virgin and whore that complicates the final rejection of the courtesan and her ultimate exclusion from the play's comic conclusion'.[24] In many ways these characters are two sides of the

---

[24] Nancy Copeland, ' "Once a whore and ever"? Whore and virgin in *The Rover* and its antecedents', *Restoration: Studies in English Literary Culture 1660–1700* 16 (1992), 21.

same coin: both advertise their attractions to Willmore and pursue him in different fashions; both are willing to subsidise his poverty with money from the same source (Hellena's fortune comes from her uncle who was Angellica's 'Spanish general'); and both offer themselves to him for love. They differ mainly in the way they view that concept in relationships between men and women. Ironically, the worldly courtesan is less astute than the convent girl in assessing the nature of a rover like Willmore. In depriving Angellica of her man, Behn is not taking a moral stand: Angellica, the romantic, must give way to Hellena, the realist, who will provide her revenge. Angellica's future is left undetermined. The opportunity Behn gives her to express herself so eloquently and the sympathy this provokes on her behalf are apt reminders that love, like carnival madness, has its darker side – and that, in carnival, everyone has a voice.

THE PLAY IN PERFORMANCE

The most popular of Aphra Behn's plays, *The Rover* has all the stock ingredients of Restoration drama – an attractive libertine, a spirited heroine, a domineering quasi-parental figure to be thwarted, and a foolish but endearing fop, trying unsuccessfully to be a rake. Florinda and Belvile's love-match, opposed by family and rival suitors, belongs to an old dramatic tradition, as does Callis's role of the governess or nurse who becomes involved in the young people's attempts to procure happiness. Angellica Bianca leaves the traditional stereotype of a prostitute behind and becomes a complex version of the dangerous scorned mistress. Yet, for all these recognisable characteristics and the usual incorporation of songs, music, sword-play, and dancing which an audience might expect from a play of this period, *The Rover* is full of surprises. On the surface, Behn appears to be working within the literary conventions of her day, but under it she pushes their boundaries as far as she dares.

Behn's first plays, *The Forced Marriage* (1670) and *The Amorous Prince* (1671), were performed by the Duke's Company at Lincoln's Inn Fields, but *The Dutch Lover* (1673), the tragedy *Abdelazer*, and the comedy *The Town Fop* (both 1676), *The Debauchee* and *The Counterfeit Bridegroom* (both attributed to Behn and dated 1677), and *The Rover* (1677) were produced at Christopher Wren's Duke's Theatre,[25] Dorset Garden, as were all her later

[25] Simon Trussler in *An Adaptation of The Rover by Aphra Behn*, London, 1986, p.11. Edward A. Langhans suggests Robert Hooke as designer of The Duke's Theatre in *LTW*, p.62.

plays until *The Lucky Chance* (1686) and *The Emperor of the Moon* (1687) came out at Drury Lane. *The Widow Ranter* and *The Younger Brother* were both produced there posthumously, in 1689 and 1696 respectively.

Restoration theatres were smaller than the vast Elizabethan and Jacobean public playhouses, seating up to approximately 800 people.[26] The Duke's Theatre, Dorset Garden, had a proscenium stage and an acting space which extended forward from the curtain line, with doors and balcony spaces on both sides. Most of the action probably took place on the forestage, nearest the audience. Reconstructions of the theatre by Edward A. Langhans suggest that this area was 19'6" (5.9 metres) deep, with a proscenium width of 30'6" (9.3 metres) and a total stage depth of 51' (15.5 metres).[27] Apart from the introduction of women to act female parts, the main advance in the Restoration period was painted background scenery, moved along grooves or tracks by machines. There would be a number of these shutters together, so that one pair could be drawn back to reveal another in place behind them and so change the setting, for example from one street to another, as at IV.iv. Behind the shutters was a discovery space, where characters could be 'discovered' or revealed: for example, the opening stage direction of IV.i. reads, '*A fine room. Discovers* BELVILE *as by dark alone*'. The shutters and the area behind them constitute the 'scene' and at IV.iii. 68 we find the stage direction '*Enter FLORINDA from the farther end of the scene, looking behind her*'. The space behind the shutters could be extended right to the back wall of the theatre to create 'long' scenes, using wings to form a perspective converging on the farthest wall. Either this or a perspective painting of a street would have been used for the 'long street' specified at I.ii. and II.i.

It was common to have a large, mechanically-operated trapdoor upstage, to raise or lower properties such as the bed in III.iii., but Dorset Garden was relatively unusual in being able to darken its stage, perhaps by lowering the footlights below stage level. This effect may have been reserved for spectacles such as occurred in Dryden and Davenant's version of *The Tempest*,[28] and may not have been in general use, but the impact of Florinda's encounter with the drunken Willmore, for example, would have differed depending on whether the audience could see actions and expressions clearly (which seems most likely),or whether

---

[26.] See J.L. Styan, *Restoration Comedy in Performance*, Cambridge, 1986, pp.20-1.

[27.] *LTW, p.62*

[28.] This was Shadwell's operatic production at Dorset Garden in 1674. See Colin Visser, 'Scenery and technical design' in *LTW*, p. 113.

the impression was one of voices and an indistinct scuffle. The usual practice in theatres at this time was to keep both stage and houselights fully operational throughout a performance and to suggest darkness on-stage through the use of candles or torches, as employed later in III.v (e.g. '*Enter* PEDRO...*with lights*', l.87). Willmore's, 'by this light' (l.16) is an asseverative phrase, i.e. 'by this [good] light', which refers to the moon: he is not carrying a lantern.

The first recorded performance of *The Rover* at the Duke's Theatre was on 24 March 1677 and Charles II was present. The play was a success, being revived at court in 1680, 1685, 1687, and 1690, and at either Drury Lane or Dorset Garden in 1685. It remained popular after Behn's death: 165 performances are recorded between 1700 and 1790.[29] After this it reappeared as *Love in Many Masks*, a toned-down version by John Philip Kemble in 1790, which indicates that theatrical tastes had changed. Behn's play appears to have been out of favour in the nineteenth century, and was neglected for the majority of the twentieth century, despite Montague Summers' edition in 1915. The Feminist Movement, which focused attention on the works of hitherto forgotten women writers, eventually brought *The Rover* back to prominence, but its first major twentieth-century production was due to the opening of a Royal Shakespeare Theatre Company venue dedicated to staging a more comprehensive range of sixteenth- and seventeenth-century plays than had been possible previously.

In 1986, John Barton, like Kemble, thought there was a need to rework Behn's text, and he produced his own edition by cutting 550 lines, adding 350 (some of these came from *Thomaso*, but others he supplied himself), and rearranging the structure and setting.[30] The new Swan Theatre at Stratford on Avon, where Barton's production was first performed in July 1986, despite the lack of a proscenium arch and painted 'scenes', may have reproduced some staging conditions similar to Dorset Garden, putting actors and audience in intimate proximity, providing a side balcony for Angellica, a trap door for Blunt, and a stage full of energetic women (Imogen Stubbs played Hellena; Geraldine Fitgerald, Florinda; and Sinead Cusack, Angellica). However, by transforming Belvile into 'a black

[29] William van Lennep, ed., *Index to The London Stage, 1660 -1880*, Carbondale and Edwardsville, 1979, p. 61

[30] John Barton, *An Adaptation of The Rover by Aphra Behn*; programme /text with commentary by Simon Trussler, Methuen, 1986. See also Nancy Copeland, 'Re-Producing *The Rover*: John Barton's *Rover* at the Swan', *Essays in Theatre* 9 (1990), 45-60.

soldier of fortune', setting the play in an unnamed Spanish colony, expanding several characters' roles (most notably that of Valeria, who became the sister of Hellena and Florinda), and altering   both the beginning and the ending, this version differed from Behn's in important ways.

By reverting to Killigrew's opening scene, Barton focused initially on male interests   rather than female. Jeremy Irons' swashbuckling Willmore looked every inch the pirate but, for some his 'flourishing first entrance' exaggerated 'the potential, which certainly exists in Behn's play, for glorification of the rover'.[31] Although Hellena claims she finds Willmore's 'unconstant humour' attractive (IV.ii.208-9), a modern audience may be less willing to indulge his urges to pounce on any young female he encounters, and more inclined to agree with the exasperated Belvile when he demands, 'Must you be a beast - a brute, a senseless swine?' (III. vi. 3). This production played the assaults on Florinda primarily for comic effect, choosing not to assert that Behn's rover is a drunken would-be rapist (III.v) and a hot-headed blunderer (IV.ii.93), as well as a tarnished hero. Similarly, Barton rearranged the ending so that it was almost a case of *Oronooko* meets *The Three [Restoration] Musketeers*. Before Belvile's final couplets to King Charles and the future marriages came the stage direction: '*All shed their Carnival gear, the Masquers all appearing as slaves and such like, and go out singing a working song*'. As a festive comedy, this version had many strengths and was highly enjoyable to watch, but it was not Behn's play. Nevertheless, the production was a success and transferred to the Mermaid Theatre, London.

Barton's text continues to be performed and, in the last twenty years, *The Rover* has appeared on stages all over the world in a variety of productions. These include those by the State Theatre Company of Australia (1989 and 1990), the Mercury Theatre Auckland, New Zealand (1989), and the New Cross Theatre, Goldsmiths College (1991). The latter was particularly successful in demonstrating Behn's ambivalent portrayal of Willmore, and stressed the lack of safety, for both men and women, in an environment where danger and violence are commonplace. Today it is hard to ignore the play's sinister elements. Elizabeth Schafer notes that, 'In Gale Edward's production of *The Rover* (State Theatre Company of South Australia, 1989 and 1990) Willmore was sometimes booed and hissed'[32] - and in a production by the Women's Playhouse Trust at London's

---

[31.] Elizabeth Schafer, 'Appropriating Aphra', *Australasian Drama Studies* 19 (1991), 43

[32.] Ibid., 49

Jacob Street Film Studios in October 1994, the tension created
in IV.v, as both Blunt and Frederick prepared to rape Florinda,
proved that though the audience knew them to be foolish and
inexperienced comic characters, it could not banish the deep
unease which their actions provoked.

Even so, this production was not as feminist as might have
been expected; the male characters were treated sympathetical-
ly even when most undeserving, with the emphasis on male
weaknesses rather than vindictiveness. This is true to the way
Behn demonstrates both an awareness of male injustice to
women and an acknowledgement of female attraction to fickle
men. However, she provokes most laughter at the expense of
her male characters. *The Rover* frequently places vulnerable
men and women in enclosed interiors (Florinda and Hellena in
I.i, Angellica in II.ii, Belvile in IV.i, Blunt in IV. v, and Florinda
in IV.v and V.i), and the vast circus ring of London's Jacob
Street Film Studios was less effective in this respect than a traditional theatre space, until the scenes concerning Blunt and
Florinda. In these, huge nets were let down from the roof to
form four walls, and first Blunt, then Florinda found themselves trapped like helpless animals in a cage or insects in a web.
Florinda's unfortunate attempt to take refuge in Blunt's chamber became a visual reminder that   the 'cobweb door set
open...to catch flies' (which, earlier, Willmore had ironically
associated with Florinda in a predatory role, III.v. 59-60) can
snare naive virgins as well as sexually-tempted men like Blunt.

The WPT production (in association with the Open
University and the BBC) was geared both to exploring the text
in ways which were relevant to a multi-cultural society, and to
making it available on stage and on video. The most striking
aspect of the performance was the ease with which the play
appeared able to accommodate and represent a number of different cultures simultaneously. On one hand, Behn is specific in
her references to the English, Spanish, and Italians, and the
play is a lively exposé of the English in Europe in the 1650s. On
the other hand, her understanding of life in a society compris-
ing such disparate groups of individuals, and her perception
concerning male-female relations, allow *The Rover* to transcend
historical and geographical restrictions. The Women's
Playhouse Trust set their production in India: it encompassed a
wide range of black cultures and an 'English' band with a variety of accents, including Irish.

There were weaknesses: a thick carpet of sand suggested heat
and a holiday sense of the exotic, but the clouds of dust which
rose whenever a rickshaw bowled past or a fight took place were
a challenge for both actors and audience. Nevertheless, the pio-

neering spirit of *The Rover* remained triumphant. One of the leading Kathakali dancers in India, Maya Krishna Rao, played Angellica as a sensuous temptress in a pavilion created beneath a floating purple veil. Her seduction techniques could hardly have differed more from those of Cecilia Noble's Hellena, as she raced around the arena on a bicycle in pursuit of Willmore. In staging *The Rover* the WPT demonstrated that it is possible to bring an exciting celebration of carnival and a meaningful exploration of gender and social issues together.

Over ten years later, *The Rover*'s appeal appears to be undiminished with numerous performances worldwide in 2005.[33] One of the most innovative of these was an adaptation by Josh Costello, who also directed it for the Chance Theater in Anaheim, California.[34] In this, Behn's play (with some cuts, a few lines from *Thomaso*, and even a couple from Shakespeare's plays in the introduction) was enacted by four 15 year old girls on a sleepover or slumber party, who used their imaginations and what they had to hand – a dressing-up chest and some dolls and puppets. Their skilled manipulation of the latter unexpectedly brought Don Pedro to life as a dog with long drooping ears and a serious expression, while Barbie and Ken dolls were effectively used to dramatise Blunt's encounter with Lucetta. Alex Bueno, Emily Clark, Vanessa Martinez and Barbara Suiter leapt in and out of their shared bunk beds (poised on top of low bookshelves), donning masks, wigs, and makeshift costumes to transport their audience back to Behn's time, occasionally breaking the spell to demonstrate the way the girls were taken over by their imaginations. Despite the lively humour that pervaded this production and the all-female cast, the potential threat of rape in III.v was menacingly conveyed. In its novel exploration of gender roles and the female imagination, Costello's thought-provoking adaptation marks another successful transformation of *The Rover* on the contemporary stage.

[33.] 2005 productions include those of the Centurion Theatre Company (London), Magdalen College (Oxford), the Royal Welsh College of Music and Drama, the University of Alberta Studio Theatre, Kalamazoo College, Michigan, the Humber School of Creative and Performing Arts, California, and Josh Costello's adaptation for the Chance Theater, Orange County, California.

[34.] The Chance Theater also produced a television broadcast for KOCE-TV. See www.joshcostello.com for more details of his adaptation.

NOTE ON THE TEXT

The first Quarto was the only edition of *The Rover* to be printed during Aphra Behn's lifetime and forms the basis for subsequent quarto editions in 1697 (Q2) and 1709 (Q3), an octavo printed in 1737, a duodecimo in 1741, and a reworking by Kemble in 1790. A two-volume collected edition of Aphra Behn's plays, based on Q2, appeared in 1702 (C) and was reissued in a single volume in 1716. A further edition in four volumes (C2) came out in 1724 and was the basis of two more editions in 1871 and 1915. Until Frederick M. link's useful edition in 1967, which went back to the authoritative first Quarto, *The Rover* had been reproduced for centuries in a variety of corrupt texts. The present edition is based on the first Quarto, and any substantive variations from it are recorded in the textual notes. Not all variants from Q2, Q3, C and C2 are listed, but any which offer plausible alternative readings are included. The original spelling of characters' names is retained, though in some cases this has had to be regularised; other spellings have been modernised, as has punctuation, but substantive variations from Q1 are noted. Q1 employs a large number of dashes, sometimes in lieu of stops or semi-colons: where applicable, substitutions have been made. Dashes have been retained where they may signify pauses in delivery (perhaps to accommodate unspecified stage business, e.g. I.i.19–22, where Hellena may pause, both for a response and to intensify Florinda's embarrasement; of I.ii.63, where Belvile may embrace Willmore), give emphasis to a final phrase (e.g. I.ii.168), indicate hesitation as a character thinks aloud (e.g. III.i.260), signal an abrupt change in addressee (e.g. I.i.64), or indicate an interrupted speech (e.g. III.i.279 and 281).

Q1's lineation is often idiosyncratic. Where the verse is very irregular and there is a precedent for setting it as prose in subsequent editions, this practice has been followed and changes from Q1 noted. Occasionally Q1 sets lines as prose when they could be verse and, again, adjustments have been made and changes noted. All editorial stage directions are in square brackets; others are as in Q1, and any changes in positioning are noted. Stage directions for entrances and exits in Q1 sometimes accommodate stage business involving other characters during the act of entering or exiting. These directions are retained, but occasional interventions have been necessary to clarify who is entering or exiting and who is merely involved in the accompanying stage actions. Speech prefixes have been written in full, though often abbreviated in Q1. Notes are supplied with the first use of a word or phrase. Subsequently, unless the context has changed, cross-references are made only from the first recurrence of the term in each act.

FURTHER READING

Altaba-Artal, Dolors, *Aphra Behn's English Feminism: Wit and Satire*, Selinsgrove, Pa., 1999

Beach, Adam R., 'Carnival politics, generous satire, and nationalist spectacle in Behn's *The Rover*', *Eighteenth-Century Life* 28 (2004), 1-19

Cameron, W.J., *New Light on Aphra Behn*, Auckland, 1961

Canfield, J. Douglas, *Tricksters and Estates: On the Ideology of Restoration Comedy*, Lexington, 1997

Carlson, Susan, 'Cannibalizing and carnivalizing: reviving Aphra Behn's *The Rover*', *Theatre Journal* 47 (1995), 517-39

Caywood, Cynthia L., 'Deconstructing Aphras: Aphra Behn and her Biographers', *Restoration: Studies in Eighteenth Century Culture* 24 (1) (2000), 15-34

Copeland, Nancy, '"Once a whore and ever"? Whore and virgin in *The Rover* and its antecedents', *Restoration: Studies in English Literary Culture 1600-1700*, 16, 1992, 20-27

Cotton, Nancy, *Women Playwrights in England, 1363-1750*, Lewisburg, 1980

Day, Robert A., 'Aphra Behn's First Biography', *Studies in Bibliography*, 22, 1969, 227-240

De Ritter, J., 'The gypsy, the rover, and the wanderer: Aphra Behn's revision of Thomas Killigrew', *Restoration: Studies in English Literary Culture 1600-1700*, 10, 1986, 82-92

Diamond, Elin, 'Gestus and signature in Aphra Behn's *The Rover*', *ELH*, 56 (1), 1989, 519-41

Duchovnay, Gerald, 'Aphra Behn's religion', *Notes and Queries*, 221, 1976, 235-37

Duffy, Maureen, *The Pasionate Shepherdess: Aphra Behn, 1640-89*, London, 1977, 2nd ed. 1989

Franceschina, John, 'Shadow and substance in Aphra Behn's *The Rover*: the semiotics of Restoration performance', *Restoration: Studies in English Literary Culture 1660-1700* 19 (1995), 29-42

Gallagher, Catherine, 'Who was that masked woman? The prostitute and the playwright in the comedies of Aphra Behn', *Women's Studies*, 15, 1988, 23-42

Goreau, Angeline, *Reconstructing Aphra*, Oxford, 1980

Hughes, Derek and Todd, Janet, eds., *The Cambridge Companion to Aphra Behn*, Cambridge, 2004

Hughes, Derek, *The Theatre of Aphra Behn*, Basingstoke, 2001

Hutner, Heidi, ed., *Rereading Aphra Behn: History, Theory, and Criticism*, Charlottesville and London, 1993

FURTHER READING

Jones, Jane, 'New light on the background and early life of Aphra Behn', *Notes and Queries*, 235, 1990, 288-93

Kreis-Schinck, Annette, *Women, Writing, and the Theater in the Early Modern Period: the Plays of Aphra Behn and Susan Centlivre*, Madison, N.J., 2001

Link, Frederick, *Aphra Behn*, New York, 1968

Lussier, Mark, '"The vile merchandize of Fortune": women, economy, and desire in Aphra Behn', *Women's Studies*, 18, 1991, 379-93

Mendelson, Sara Heller, 'Aphra Behn', in *The Mental World of Stuart Women: Three Studies*, Brighton, 1987

Musser, Joseph F. Jr., '"Imposing nought but constancy in love": Aphra Behn snares the rover', *Restoration:Studies in English Literary Culture 1600-1700*, 3 (1), 1979, 17-25

O'Donnell, Mary Ann, *Aphra Behn: An Annotated Bibliography of Primary and Secondary Sources*, New York, 1986

O'Donnell, Mary Ann, 'Tory wit and unconventional woman: Aphra Behn' in *Women Writers of the Seventeenth Century*, eds. Katharina M. Wilson & Frank J. Warnke , Athens, Ga., 1989, pp. 341-74

Owens, W.R. and Goodman, L., eds., *Shakespeare, Aphra Behn and the Canon*, London, 1996

Pacheco, Anita, 'Rape and the female subject in Aphra Behn's *The Rover*', *ELH* 65 (2) (1998), 323-46

Pearson, Jacqueline, *The Prostituted Muse: Images of Women and Women Dramatists, 1642-1737*, New York, 1988

Schafer, Elizabeth, 'Appropriating Aphra', *Australasian Drama Studies*, 19 (1991), 39-49

Spencer, Jane, *Aphra Behn's Afterlife*, Oxford, 2000

Szilagyi, Stephen, 'The sexual politics of Behn's *Rover*: after patriarchy', *Studies in Philology* 95 (4) (1998), 435-56

Taetzsch, Lynne, 'Romantic love replaces kinship exchange in Aphra Behn's Restoration drama', Restoration: *Studies in English Literary Culture 1660-1700*, 17, 1993, 30-38

Todd, Janet, *Aphra Behn*, Basingstoke, 1999

Todd, Janet, *Aphra Behn Studies*, Cambridge, 1996

Todd, Janet, *The Secret Life of Aphra Behn*, London, 1996

Todd, Janet, ed., *The Works of Aphra Behn*, 7 vols., London, 1992-96

Weber, Harold, *The Restoration Rake-hero: Transformations in Sexual Understanding in Seventeenth-century England*, Madison, 1986

Wiseman, S.J., *Aphra Behn*, Plymouth, 1996

THE
ROVER.
OR,
𝕿𝖍𝖊 𝕭𝖆𝖓𝖎𝖘𝖍'𝖙 𝕮𝖆𝖛𝖆𝖑𝖎𝖊𝖗𝖘.

As it is ACTED

AT

𝕳𝖎𝖘 𝕽𝖔𝖞𝖆𝖑 𝕳𝖎𝖌𝖍𝖓𝖊𝖘

THE

Duke's Theatre.

Licenfed *July* 2^d. 1677.

ROGER L'ESTRANGE.

LONDON,

Printed for *John Amery,* at the *Peacock,* againſt
St. *Dunſtan's* Church in *Fleet-ſtreet.* 1677.

Reproduction by kind permission of the British Library

PROLOGUE

Wits, like physicians, never can agree,
When of a different society.
And Rabel's drops were never more cried down
By all the learned doctors of the town,
Than a new play whose author is unknown.   5
Nor can those doctors with more malice sue
(And powerful purses) the dissenting few,
Than those, with an insulting pride, do rail
At all who are not of their own cabal.
  If a young poet hit your humour right,   10
You judge him then out of revenge and spite.
So amongst men there are ridiculous elves,
Who monkeys hate for being too like themselves.
So that the reason of the grand debate
Why wit so oft is damned when good plays take,   15
Is that you censure as you love, or hate.
  Thus like a learned conclave poets sit,
Catholic judges both of sense and wit,
And damn or save, as they themselves think fit.
Yet those who to others' faults are so severe,   20
Are not so perfect but themselves may err.
Some write correct, indeed, but then the whole
(Bating their own dull stuff i'th' play) is stole:
As bees do suck from flowers their honey dew,
So they rob others striving to please you.   25
  Some write their characters genteel and fine,
But then they do so toil for every line,
That what to you does easy seem, and plain,
Is the hard issue of their labouring brain.
And some, th'effects of all their pains we see,   30
Is but to mimic good extempore.
Others, by long converse about the town,
Have wit enough to write a lewd lampoon,

---

  3 *Rabel's drops* a patent medicine
  9 *cabal* secret or private clique
12 *men* Q1, Q2, C, C2 (them Q3)
    elves malicious persons
18 *and wit* Q1, Q3, C, C2 (of wit Q2)
21 *themselves* Q1, Q3, C2 (they themselves Q2, C)
23 *bating* excepting

3

But their chief skill lies in a bawdy song.
In short, the only wit that's now in fashion   35
Is but the gleanings of good conversation.
As for the author of this coming play,
I asked him what he thought fit I should say
In thanks for your good company today:
He called me fool, and said it was well known   40
You came not here for our sakes, but your own.
New plays are stuffed with wits, and with debauches,
That crowd and sweat like cits in May-Day coaches.

WRITTEN BY A PERSON OF QUALITY

42 *debauches* ed. (deboches Q1)
43 *cits* citizens, ordinary people

THE PERSONS OF THE PLAY

DON ANTONIO, the viceroy's son
DON PEDRO, a noble Spaniard, his friend
FLORINDA, sister to Don Pedro
HELLENA, a gay young woman, designed for a nun, and
    sister to Florinda   5
BELVILE, an English colonel in love with Florinda
WILLMORE, the Rover
ANGELLICA BIANCA, a famous courtesan
MORETTA, her woman
BLUNT, an English country gentleman   10
FREDERICK, an English gentleman, and friend to Belvile
    and Blunt
VALERIA, a kinswoman to Florinda
CALLIS, governess to Florinda and Hellena
LUCETTA, a jilting wench   15
STEPHANO, servant to Don Pedro
PHILIPPO, Lucetta's gallant
SANCHO, pimp to Lucetta
BISKEY and SEBASTIAN, two bravos to Angellica
PAGE TO DON ANTONIO   20
Officers and soldiers
Servants; other masqueraders (men and women)

The Scene

NAPLES, *in carnival time*

---

10 Blunt Q2, C, C2 (Fred. Q1, Q3)
    Sexes segregated in Q1. See the list of 'The Actors' Names', p. 6.

The Actors Names.

Mr. *Jevorne*,	*Don Antonio*,	The Vice-Roy's Son.
Mr. *Medburne*,	*Don Pedro*,	A Noble *Spaniard*, his Friend.
Mr. *Betterton*,	*Belvile*,	An *English* Colonel in Love with *Florinda*.
Mr. *Smith*,	*Willmore*,	The *ROVER*.
Mr. *Crosbie*,	*Frederick*,	An *English* Gentleman, and Friend to *Bel.* and *Fred.*
Mr. *Underhill*,	*Blunt*,	An *English* Country Gentleman.
Mr. *Richards*,	*Stephano*,	Servant to *Don Pedro*.
Mr. *Percivall*,	*Philippo*,	*Lucetta*'s Gallant.
Mr. *John Lee*,	*Sancho*,	Pimp to *Lucetta*.
	Biskey, and *Sebastian*,	} *Two Bravo's to* Angellica.
	Officers and Souldiers.	
	Page	To *Don Antonio*.

Women.

Mrs. *Betterton*,	*Florinda*,	Sister to *Don Pedro*.
Mrs. *Barrer*,	*Hellena*,	A gay Young Woman defign'd for a Nun, and Sister to *Florinda*.
Mrs. *Hughs*,	*Valeria*,	A Kinswoman to *Florinda*.
Mrs. *Gwin*,	*Angellica Bianca*,	A Famous Courtizan.
Mrs. *Leigh*,	*Moretta*,	Her Woman.
Mrs. *Norris*,	*Callis*,	Governess to *Florinda* and *Hellena*.
Mrs. *Gillo*,	*Lucetta*,	A Jilting Wench.

Servants, Other *Masqueraders* Men and Women.

The Scene *NAPLES*, in Carnival time.

THE

THE ROVER

Act I, Scene i

A chamber
Enter FLORINDA *and* HELLENA

FLORINDA

What an impertinent thing is a young girl bred in a
nunnery! How full of questions! Prithee no more,
Hellena; I have told thee more than thou understand'st
already.

HELLENA

The more's my grief. I would fain know as much as you,   5
which makes me so inquisitive; nor is't enough I know
you're a lover, unless you tell me, too, who 'tis you sigh
for.

FLORINDA

When you're a lover I'll think you fit for a secret of that
nature.   10

HELLENA

'Tis true, I never was a lover yet – but I begin to have a
shrewd guess what 'tis to be so, and fancy it very pretty
to sigh, and sing, and blush, and wish, and dream and
wish, and long and wish to see the man; and when I do,
look pale and tremble, just as you did when my brother   15
brought home the fine English colonel to see you – what
do you call him, Don Belvile?

FLORINDA

Fie, Hellena.

HELLENA

That blush betrays you. I am sure 'tis so – or is it
Don Antonio the viceroy's son? – Or perhaps the   20
rich old Don Vincentio, whom my father designs you
for a husband? – Why do you blush again?

---

0 s.d. 1 *chamber* private room rather than bedroom

2 *Prithee* [I] pray thee

5 *fain* gladly, willingly

6 *I know* Q1 (to know Q2)

20 *viceroy* vice-king, one governing in the name and by the authority of the supreme
ruler

21–2 *designs you for a* Q1, Q3 (designs for your Q2)
designs designates, intends

FLORINDA

With indignation; and how near soever my father thinks
I am to marrying that hated object, I shall let him see I
understand better what's due to my beauty, birth, and   25
fortune, and more – to my soul, than to obey those
unjust commands.

HELLENA

Now hang me if I don't love thee for that dear dis-
obedience. I love mischief strangely, as most of our sex
do, who are come to love nothing else – but tell me, dear   30
Florinda, don't you love that fine *Anglese*? For I vow,
next to loving him myself, 'twill please me most that you
do so, for he is so gay and so handsome!

FLORINDA

Hellena, a maid designed for a nun ought not to be so
curious in a discourse of love.   35

HELLENA

And dost thou think that ever I'll be a nun? Or at least
till I'm so old, I'm fit for nothing else? Faith, no, sister;
and that which makes me long to know whether you love
Belvile, is because I hope he has some mad companion or
other that will spoil my devotion. Nay, I'm resolved to   40
provide myself this carnival, if there be e'er a handsome
proper fellow of my humour above ground, though I ask
first.

FLORINDA

Prithee be not so wild.

HELLENA

Now you have provided yourself of a man, you take no care   45
for poor me. Prithee tell me, what dost thou see about

24–6 *see I understand ... and more – to* ed. (see, I understand ... and more to Q1)
29 *strangely* very greatly
31 *Anglese* Englishman (a hybrid word, combining the French 'Anglais' with the
   Italian 'Inglese')
33 *gay* exuberantly cheerful
34 *designed* intended
40 *spoil* make spoil of, i.e. plunder her devotion for himself
41 *provide* furnish, equip
   carnival from the Italian 'carne levare': the putting away of flesh as food (*OED*);
   festivity prior to the forty days of Lent when Catholics abstained from eating
   meat, characterised by freedom from social restrictions and the indulgence of the
   body
42 *proper* 1) fine 2) honest, respectable
   humour disposition
42–3 *though ... first* even if I have to take the initiative
45 *of a man* Q1 (with a man Q2)

me that is unfit for love? Have I not a world of youth? A
humour gay? A beauty passable? A vigour desirable?
Well shaped? Clean limbed? Sweet breathed? And sense
enough to know how all these ought to be employed to   50
the best advantage? Yes, I do and will. Therefore lay
aside your hopes of my fortune by my being a devotee,
and tell me how you came acquainted with this Belvile;
for I perceive you knew him before he came to Naples.

FLORINDA
Yes, I knew him at the siege of Pamplona; he was then   55
a colonel of French horse, who when the town was
ransacked, nobly treated my brother and myself, preserving us from all insolences; and I must own, besides
great obligations, I have I know not what that pleads
kindly for him about my heart, and will suffer no other   60
to enter. – But see, my brother.

Enter DON PEDRO [*and*] STEPHANO, *with a masquing habit,*
and CALLIS

PEDRO
Good morrow, sister. Pray, when saw you your lover
Don Vincentio?

FLORINDA
I know not, sir. – Callis, when was he here? For I consider
it so little, I know not when it was.   65

PEDRO
I have a command from my father here, to tell you you
ought not to despise him, a man of so vast a fortune,
and such a passion for you. – Stephano, my things.

Puts on his masquing habit

FLORINDA
A passion for me! 'Tis more than e'er I saw, or he had a

---

52 *devotee* ed. (devote Q1) a religious zealot, a nun – with, perhaps, a mischievous
   allusion to the practice of using religious vocabulary for the erotic in the language
   of French courtly love
55 *Pamplona* ed. (Pampulona Q1) the strongly fortified capital of Navarre
56 *horse* cavalry. He is an exile, hired for foreign service.
61 s.d. 1 *masquing habit* set of clothes for a masquerade; i.e. an elaborate mask and
   disguise
62 *lover* suitor
66–7 *father here, … you you ought* ed. (Father here … you, you ought Q1)
68 *my things* Q1 (m'thinks – Q2)

desire should be known. I hate Vincentio, sir, and I   70
would not have a man so dear to me as my brother follow
the ill customs of our country and make a slave of his
sister. – And sir, my father's will, I'm sure you may
divert.

PEDRO

I know not how dear I am to you, but I wish only to be   75
ranked in your esteem, equal with the English Colonel
Belvile. Why do you frown and blush? Is there any guilt
belongs to the name of that cavalier?

FLORINDA

I'll not deny I value Belvile: when I was exposed to such
dangers as the licensed lust of common soldiers   80
threatened when rage and conquest flew through the
city – then Belvile, this criminal for my sake, threw
himself into all dangers to save my honour – and will
you not allow him my esteem?

PEDRO

Yes, pay him what you will in honour – but you must   85
consider Don Vincentio's fortune, and the jointure he'll
make you.

FLORINDA

Let him consider my youth, beauty, and fortune; which
ought not to be thrown away on his age and jointure.

PEDRO

'Tis true, he's not so young and fine a gentleman as that   90
Belvile – but what jewels will that cavalier present you
with? Those of his eyes and heart?

HELLENA

And are not those better than any Don Vincentio has
brought from the Indies?

PEDRO

Why how now! Has your nunnery-breeding taught you   95
to understand the value of hearts and eyes?

HELLENA

Better than to believe Vincentio's deserve value from

---

78 *cavalier* 1) horse-soldier 2) one who fought for Charles I against Parliament
79–81 *such dangers . . . threatened* sexual violation of women traditionally allowed to
   the victors
82 *criminal . . . sake* Belvile took Florinda's side against his own men.
   threw Q3 (through Q1)
86 *jointure* estate settled on a wife, to be enjoyed by her after her husband's death

any woman. He may perhaps increase her bags, but not
her family.

PEDRO

This is fine! Go – up to your devotion. You are not   100
designed for the conversation of lovers.

HELLENA (*Aside*)

Nor saints, yet a while, I hope. [*To Pedro*] – Is't not
enough you make a nun of me, but you must cast my
sister away too, exposing her to a worse confinement
than a religious life?   105

PEDRO

The girl's mad. It is a confinement to be carried into the
country, to an ancient villa belonging to the family of
the Vincentios these five hundred years, and have no
other prospect than that pleasing one of seeing all her
own that meets her eyes – a fine air, large fields and   110
gardens, where she may walk and gather flowers!

HELLENA

When by moon-light? For I am sure she dares not
encounter with the heat of the sun; that were a task only
for Don Vincentio and his Indian breeding, who loves it
in the dog-days. And if these be her daily divert-   115
issements, what are those of the night? To lie in a wide
moth-eaten bed-chamber with furniture in fashion in
the reign of King Sancho the First; the bed, that which
his forefathers lived and died in.

PEDRO

Very well.   120

HELLENA

This apartment – new furbished and fitted out for the
young wife – he, out of freedom, makes his dressing
room; and being a frugal and a jealous coxcomb, instead
of a valet to uncase his feeble carcass, he desires you to
do that office – signs of favour, I'll assure you, and such   125

98 *bags* money bags, with a jibe at Vincentio's supposed lack of virility ('to bag'
could also mean 'to make pregnant')

100 *fine! Go – up* ed. (fine – go – up Q1)

106 *it is* Q1 (is it Q3)

109 *prospect* 1) view 2) expectation

115 *dog-days* the days when the Dog-star rises (traditionally the hottest and most
unwholesome time of the year, associated with malignant influences)

115–16 *divertissements* entertainments

118 *King Sancho the First* Sancho I Garces, King of Navarre (Pamplona) from 905

121 *furbished* ed. (furbrusht Q1) renovated

123 *coxcomb* fool

124 *uncase* undress

Handwritten margin note: Hellena's presentation of marriage subverts the traditional depiction

as you must not hope for, unless your woman be out of
the way.

PEDRO

Have you done yet?

HELLENA

That honour being past, the giant stretches himself,
yawns and sighs a belch or two, loud as a musket –   130
throws himself into bed, and expects you in his foul
sheets, and e'er you can get yourself undressed, calls
you with a snore or two – and are not these fine blessings
to a young lady?

PEDRO

Have you done yet?   135

HELLENA

And this man you must kiss, nay you must kiss none but
him, too – and nuzzle through his beard to find his lips –
and this you must submit to for threescore years, and
all for a jointure.

PEDRO

For all your character of Don Vincentio, she is as like to   140
marry him as she was before.

HELLENA

Marry Don Vincentio! Hang me, such a wedlock would
be worse than adultery with another man. I had rather
see her in the *Hostel de Dieu*, to waste her youth there in
vows and be a handmaid to lazars and cripples, than to   145
lose it in such a marriage.

PEDRO

You have considered, sister, that Belvile has no fortune
to bring to you, banished his country, despised at home,
and pitied abroad?

HELLENA

What then? The viceroy's son is better than that old Sir   150
Fisty. Don Vincentio! Don Indian! He thinks he's trading

---

129 *himself* Q3 (itself Q1)
130 *loud* Q1 (as loud C)
140 *character ... Vincentio* description of Don Vincentio's qualities
144 *Hostel de Dieu* (usually medieval) hospital run by a religious order
145 *lazars* poor and diseased people, especially lepers
148 *to you* ed. (you to Q1)
150–1 *Sir Fisty* Q1 is unclear; this may read 'Fisty' or 'Fifty' (Fifty Q3; Fisty C;
       unclear C2). If 'Fifty', Hellena is making a tame jibe at Vincentio's age; if 'Fisty',
       it is a play on 'fist' (v2 *OED*), meaning 'to break wind'.

to Gambo still, and would barter himself – that bell and
bauble – for your youth and fortune.

PEDRO

Callis, take her hence, and lock her up all this carnival,
and at Lent she shall begin her everlasting penance in a   155
monastery.

HELLENA

I care not. I had rather be a nun than be obliged to
marry as you would have me, if I were designed for't.

PEDRO

Do not fear the blessing of that choice. You shall be a
nun.   160

HELLENA (*Aside*)

Shall I so? You may chance to be mistaken in my way of
devotion – a nun! Yes, I am like to make a fine nun! I
have an excellent humour for a grate. No, I'll have a
saint of my own to pray to shortly, if I like any that dares
venture on me.   165

PEDRO

Callis, make it your business to watch this wild cat. As
for you, Florinda, I've only tried you all this while and
urged my father's will – but mine is, that you would
love Antonio; he is brave and young, and all that can
complete the happiness of a gallant maid. This absence   170
of my father will give us opportunity to free you from
Vincentio by marrying here, which you must do tomorrow.

[handwritten margin note: Pedro is boss taking control of his sisters.]

FLORINDA

Tomorrow!

PEDRO

Tomorrow, or 'twill be too late – 'tis not my friendship   175
to Antonio which makes me urge this, but love to thee
and hatred to Vincentio – therefore resolve upon tomorrow.

---

152 *Gambo* Gambia, West Africa, supplying less exotic trading opportunities than
    the Gold Coast, further south. The West-African slave trade began to boom in
    the middle of the seventeenth century.

152–3 *bell and bauble* trifle (like the worthless objects offered to indigenous peoples
    by some European traders in return for items of great value)

155 *Lent* in the Christian church, a time of penance in preparation for Easter. See
    Breughel's painting *The Battle of Carnival and Lent*.

163 *grate* a framework of bars fixed in a door or window to allow restricted com-
    munication

167 *tried* tested

FLORINDA
  Sir, I shall strive to do as shall become your sister.
PEDRO
  I'll both believe and trust you. Adieu.   180
                          Exeunt PEDRO *and* STEPHANO
HELLENA
  As becomes his sister! That is to be as resolved your way
  as he is his.

                    HELLENA *goes to* CALLIS

FLORINDA
  I ne'er till now perceived my ruin near.
  I've no defence against Antonio's love,
  For he has all the advantages of nature,   185
  The moving arguments of youth and fortune.
HELLENA
  But hark you, Callis, you will not be so cruel to lock me
  up indeed, will you?
CALLIS
  I must obey the commands I have. Besides, do you
  consider what a life you are going to lead?   190
HELLENA
  Yes, Callis, that of a nun: and till then I'll be indebted a
  world of prayers to you if you'll let me now see what I
  never did, the divertissements of a carnival.
CALLIS
  What, go in masquerade? 'Twill be a fine farewell to the
  world, I take it. Pray what would you do there?   195
HELLENA
  That which all the world does, as I am told – be as mad
  as the rest and take all innocent freedoms. – Sister, you'll
  go too, will you not? Come prithee be not sad. We'll
  outwit twenty brothers if you'll be ruled by me. Come
  put off this dull humour with your clothes, and assume   200
  one as gay, and as fantastic as the dress my cousin Valeria
  and I have provided, and let's ramble.
FLORINDA
  Callis, will you give us leave to go?
CALLIS (*Aside*)
  I have a youthful itch of going myself.
  – Madam, if I thought your brother might not know it,   205

---

189 *have* Q1, Q3 (hate Q2, C, C2)
202 *ramble* roam in a free and unrestrained fashion (with sexual resonances of lib-
    ertine behaviour)

and I might wait on you; for, by my troth, I'll not trust
young girls alone.
FLORINDA
Thou see'st my brother's gone already, and thou shalt
attend and watch us.

Enter STEPHANO

STEPHANO
Madam, the habits are come, and your cousin Valeria   210
is dressed and stays for you.
FLORINDA
'Tis well. I'll write a note, and if I chance to see Belvile
and want an opportunity to speak to him, that shall let
him know what I've resolved in favour of him.
HELLENA
Come, let's in and dress us.   215

Exeunt

[Act I,] Scene ii

A long street
Enter BELVILE, *melancholy,* BLUNT *and* FREDERICK

FREDERICK
Why, what the devil ails the colonel in a time when all
the world is gay, to look like mere Lent thus? Hadst thou
been long enough in Naples to have been in love, I
should have sworn some such judgement had befallen
thee.   5
BELVILE
No, I have made no new amours since I came to Naples.
FREDERICK
You have left none behind you in Paris?
BELVILE
Neither.
FREDERICK
I cannot divine the cause then, unless the old cause, the
want of money. — mamidge a money institution.   10

210 *Madam,* Q3 (Mad? Q1)
    habits costumes
211 *stays* waits
  1 *Why, . . . colonel in* ed. (Whe what . . . Devil ails the Coll. In Q1) The exclamation
    'whe' occurs frequently in Q1 and has been emended to 'why' throughout. Todd
    notes that 'whe' 'suggests a stronger tone than "why" possesses' (T, p. 364).
  6 *amours* romantic liaisons
 10 *want* lack

BLUNT

And another old cause, the want of a wench. Would not
that revive you?

BELVILE

You are mistaken, Ned.

BLUNT

Nay, 'sheartlikins, then thou'rt past cure.

FREDERICK

I have found it out: thou hast renewed thy acquaintance   15
with the lady that cost thee so many sighs at the siege of
Pamplona. – Pox on't, what d'e you call her – her brother's a noble Spaniard, nephew to the dead general. –
Florinda! Ay, Florinda. And will nothing serve thy turn
but that damned virtuous woman, whom on my con-   20
science thou lov'st in spite too, because thou seest little
or no possibility of gaining her?

BELVILE

has given Thou art mistaken; I have int'rest enough in that lovely
up hope virgin's heart to make me proud and vain, were it not
of winning abated by the severity of a brother, who perceiving my   25
Florinda happiness –

FREDERICK

Has civilly forbid thee the house?

BELVILE

'Tis so, to make way for a powerful rival, the viceroy's
son, who has the advantage of me in being a man of
fortune, a Spaniard, and her brother's friend; which   30
gives him liberty to make his court, whilst I have recourse
only to letters, and distant looks from her window, which
are as soft and kind
As those which Heaven sends down on penitents.

BLUNT

Heyday! 'Sheartlikins, simile! By this light the man is   35
quite spoiled. – Fred, what the devil are we made of,
that we cannot be thus concerned for a wench? 'Sheartlikins, our Cupids are like the cooks of the camp – they

---

14 *'sheartlikins* from ''adsheartlikins'. 'Ads' is a variant of 'ods', a minced form of
   'God's'; 'heartlikin', or 'little heart', is a term of endearment: the expression
   becomes characteristic of Blunt.

23–4 *int'rest … heart* stake (share) … affections

31 *liberty … court* freedom to carry out his courtship openly

34 *As … penitents* Q1 changes from prose to verse here.

36–7 *– Fred … wench?* ed. (*– Fred. … Wench –* Q1) '*Fred.*' may be a speech prefix
   in Q1, but the lines are set within Blunt's speech. The dash after 'Wench' indicates
   that a further speech prefix for Blunt may have been accidentally omitted.

can roast or boil a woman, but they have none of the
fine tricks to set 'em off – no hogoes to make the sauce   40
pleasant, and the stomach sharp.

FREDERICK
I dare swear I have had a hundred as young, kind, and
handsome as this Florinda; and dogs eat me, if they were
not as troublesome to me i'th' morning as they were
welcome o'er night.   45

BLUNT
And yet, I warrant, he would not touch another woman,
if he might have her for nothing.

BELVILE
That's thy joy, a cheap whore.

BLUNT
Why, 'sheartlikins, I love a frank soul. When did you
ever hear of an honest woman that took a man's money?   50
I warrant 'em good ones. But gentlemen, you may be
free; you have been kept so poor with parliaments and
protectors, that the little stock you have is not worth
preserving – but I thank my stars I had more grace than
to forfeit my estate by cavaliering.   55

BELVILE
Methinks only following the court should be sufficient
to entitle 'em to that.

BLUNT
'Sheartlikins, they know I follow it to do it no good,
unless they pick a hole in my coat for lending you money
now and then; which is a greater crime to my conscience,   60
gentlemen, than to the Commonwealth.

Enter WILLMORE

WILLMORE
Ha! Dear Belvile! Noble colonel!

BELVILE
Willmore! Welcome ashore, my dear rover! – What
happy wind blew us this good fortune?

WILLMORE
Let me salute my dear Fred, and then command me. –   65

---

40 *hogoes* piquant flavours and relishes

49 *Why,* ed. (Whe I Q1)

52–3 *parliaments and protectors* Since the imprisonment and beheading of Charles I
   in 1649, Britain was governed by Parliament under the leadership of Protectors,
   Oliver and Richard Cromwell, who confiscated many Royalist estates.

59 *pick a hole in my coat* find fault with me

61 *Commonwealth* the republican government, 1649–60

How is't, honest lad?

FREDERICK

Faith, sir, the old compliment: infinitely the better to
see my dear mad Willmore again. Prithee why camest
thou ashore? And where's the prince?

WILLMORE

He's well and reigns still Lord of the Wat'ry Element. I   70
must aboard again within a day or two, and my business
ashore was only to enjoy myself a little this carnival.

BELVILE

Pray know our new friend, sir; he's but bashful, a raw
traveller, but honest, stout, and <u>one of us</u>.

Embraces BLUNT

WILLMORE

That you esteem him gives him an int'rest here.   75

BLUNT

Your servant, sir.

WILLMORE

But well – faith I'm glad to meet you again in a warm
climate, where the kind sun has its god-like power still
over the wine and women. Love and mirth are my business in Naples! And if I mistake not the place, here's   80
an excellent market for chapmen of my humour.

love for them based upon sex

BELVILE

<u>See, here be those kind merchants of love you look for.</u>

*Enter several men in masquing habits, some playing on
music, others dancing after; women dressed like courtesans,
with papers pinned on their breasts, and baskets of flowers
in their hands*

BLUNT

'Sheartlikins, what have we here!

FREDERICK

Now the game begins.

WILLMORE

Fine pretty creatures! May a stranger have leave to look   85
and love? – What's here? (*Reads the papers*) – 'Roses for
every month'!

---

69 *prince* the exiled son of Charles I, future Charles II
81 *chapmen* itinerant dealers who buy and sell, or purchasers (as here)
82 s.d. 1 *masquing habits* See I.i.61 s.d. note.
   s.d. 2 *music* musical instruments
86 s.d. *Reads . . . papers* follows line in Q1

BLUNT

'Roses for every month'! What means that?

BELVILE

They are, or would have you think they're courtesans,
who here in Naples are to be hired by the month.   90

WILLMORE

Kind and obliging to inform us – pray where do these
roses grow? I would fain plant some of 'em in a bed of
mine.

WOMAN

Beware such roses, sir.

WILLMORE

A pox of fear: I'll be baked with thee between a pair of   95
sheets, and that's thy proper still; so I might but strew
such roses over me and under me. Fair one, would you
would give me leave to gather at your bush this idle
month; I would go near to make somebody smell of it
all the year after.   100

BELVILE

And thou hast need of such a remedy, for thou stink'st
of tar and ropes' ends like a dock or pesthouse.

*The woman puts herself into
the hands of a man and exeunt*

WILLMORE

Nay, nay, you shall not leave me so. *– agressive and violent in
his pursuit of women.*

BELVILE

By all means use no violence here.

WILLMORE

*quick to 'love'
→ a different
meaning?* Death! Just as I was going to be damnably in love, to   105
have her led off! I could pluck that rose out of his hand,
and even kiss the bed the bush grew in.

FREDERICK

No friend to love like a long voyage at sea.

BLUNT

Except a nunnery, Fred.

WILLMORE

Death! But will they not be kind? Quickly be kind? Thou   110

---

91 *Kind ... obliging* i.e. be so good as

95–100 *I'll ... after.* In distillation, the substance to be distilled is subjected to heat:
he is implying that the best kind of still is a pair of sheets containing roses like
her, with whom he would willingly be distilled into a strong perfume.

102 *dock* originally where vessels were built or brought for repair
pesthouse hospital for plague (pestilence) sufferers

103–4 The implication is that Willmore offers force – either to the woman, to pull
her to him, or to the man, by being about to draw his sword.

know'st I'm no tame sigher, but a rampant lion of the
forest.

*Advance from the farther end of the scenes, two men dressed
all over with horns of several sorts, making grimaces at one
another, with papers pinned on their backs*

BELVILE
Oh the fantastical rogues, how they're dressed! 'Tis a
satire against the whole sex.
WILLMORE
Is this a fruit that grows in this warm country?   115
BELVILE
Yes, 'tis pretty to see these Italians start, swell, and stab
at the word 'cuckold', and yet stumble at horns on every
threshold.
WILLMORE
See what's on their back. (*Reads*) 'Flowers of every
night.' Ah, rogue! And more sweet than roses of every   120
month! This is a gardener of Adam's own breeding.

                    They dance

BELVILE
What think you of those grave people? Is a wake in Essex
half so mad or extravagant?
WILLMORE
I like their sober grave way; 'tis a kind of legal authorised
fornication, where the men are not chid for't, nor the   125
women despised, as amongst our dull English. Even the
monsieurs want that part of good manners.
BELVILE
But here in Italy, a monsieur is the humblest best-bred
gentleman – duels are so baffled by bravos that an age
shows not one but between a Frenchman and a   130
hangman, who is as much too hard for him on the Piazza

---

112 s.d.1 *Advance* ed. (Advances Q1)
    the farther end of the scenes i.e. up stage
117 *horns* Traditionally it was supposed that horns grew on the forehead of a man
    with an unfaithful wife. As the traditional sign of cuckoldry, horns are the basis
    of many jokes in English comedy from Shakespeare onwards.
122 *Essex* Blunt's home ground (see II.i.44 and 86)
127 *monsieurs* Frenchmen
129 *baffled* confounded, foiled
    bravos hired ruffians, assassins
131 *Piazza* large open square

as they are for a Dutchman on the New Bridge. But see,
another crew.

Enter FLORINDA, HELLENA, *and* VALERIA, *dressed like*
gipsies; CALLIS *and* STEPHANO, LUCETTA, PHILIPPO *and*
SANCHO *in masquerade*

HELLENA

Sister, there's your Englishman, and with him a handsome proper fellow. I'll to him, and instead of telling   135
him his fortune, try my own. — out for herself — wants to
                                 escape from her fate — powerful.

WILLMORE

Gipsies, on my life. Sure these will prattle if a man cross
their hands. (*Goes to* HELLENA) – Dear, pretty, and, I
hope, young devil, will you tell an amorous stranger
what luck he's like to have?   140

doesn't realise he's playing into her hands.

HELLENA

Have a care how you venture with me, sir, lest I pick
your pocket, which will more vex your English humour
than an Italian fortune will please you. — plays innocent & meek
                                            whilst having control.

WILLMORE

How the devil cam'st thou to know my country and
humour?   145

HELLENA

The first I guess by a certain forward impudence, which
does not displease me at this time; and the loss of your
money will vex you because I hope you have but very
little to lose.

WILLMORE

Egad, child, thou'rt i'th' right; it is so little I dare not   150
offer it thee for a kindness. But cannot you divine what
other things of more value I have about me that I would
more willingly part with?

HELLENA

Indeed no, that's the business of a witch, and I am but
a gipsy yet. Yet without looking in your hand, I have   155
a parlous guess 'tis some foolish heart you mean, an
inconstant English heart, as little worth stealing as your
purse. playing a dangerous game — but her clever
       straight forward manner secures her Willmore.

132 *they* the French, who were successful in Flanders (see also II.i. 272–3 note)
133 s.d. 1–2 *dressed like gipsies* so that their faces are hidden by veils or head-dresses.
     See Willmore's comments at ll. 138–9, 330–1, and the exchange at 194–7.
137–8 *cross their hands* i.e. with silver; put money in their hands
142 *humour* temperament
150 *Egad* by God!
156 *parlous* clever

WILLMORE

Nay, then thou dost deal with the devil, that's certain.
Thou hast guessed as right as if thou hadst been one of   160
that number it has languished for. I find you'll be better
acquainted with it, nor can you take it in a better time;
for I am come from sea, child, and Venus not being
propitious to me in her own element, I have a world of
love in store. Would you would be good-natured and   165
take some on't off my hands.

HELLENA

Why, I could be inclined that way, but for a foolish vow
I am going to make – to die a maid.

WILLMORE

USES RELIGION TO GET AT HER. Then thou art damned without redemption, and as I am
a good Christian, I ought in charity to divert so wicked   170
a design. Therefore prithee, dear creature, let me know
quickly when and where I shall begin to set a helping
hand to so good a work.

HELLENA

If you should prevail with my tender heart – as I begin
to fear you will, for you have horrible loving eyes – there   175
will be difficulty in't, that you'll hardly undergo for my
sake.

WILLMORE

Bravity & trad. male role. Faith, child, I have been bred in dangers, and wear a
sword that has been employed in a worse cause than for
a handsome kind woman. Name the danger; let it be   180
anything but a long siege, and I'll undertake it.

HELLENA

Can you storm?

WILLMORE

Oh, most furiously.

HELLENA

What think you of a nunnery wall? For he that wins me
must gain that first. ~ *testing/daring him to determine*   185
                      his integrity

WILLMORE

irony of Hellena's unsaintly designs A nun! Oh, how I love thee for't! There's no sinner like
a young saint. Nay, now there's no denying me; the old
law had no curse – to a woman – like dying a maid:
witness Jephthah's daughter.

163–4 *Venus . . . element* The goddess of love came from the sea.

168 *maid* virgin

182 *storm* violently assault a fortified place

189 *Jephthah's daughter* Judges 11: 37–40: Jephthah sacrificed his daughter to keep a
   promise and for four days before being killed, she was allowed to roam and
   bemoan her virginity.

HELLENA

A very good text this, if well handled; and I perceive, 190
Father Captain, you would impose no severe penance
on her who were inclined to console herself before she
took orders.

WILLMORE

If she be young and handsome.

HELLENA

Ay, there's it. But if she be not –   195

WILLMORE

By this hand, child, I have an implicit faith, and dare
venture on thee with all faults. Besides, 'tis more meri-
torious to leave the world when thou hast tasted and
proved the pleasure on't. Then 'twill be a virtue in thee,
which now will be pure ignorance.   200

HELLENA

I perceive, good Father Captain, you design only to
make me fit for Heaven. But if, on the contrary, you
should quite divert me from it, and bring me back to
the world again, I should have a new man to seek, I find.
And what a grief that will be – for when I begin, I fancy 205
I shall love like anything; I never tried yet.

WILLMORE

Egad, and that's kind! – Prithee, dear creature, give me
credit for a heart, for faith, I'm a very honest fellow. Oh,
I long to come first to the banquet of love! And such a
swinging appetite I bring. Oh, I'm impatient. Thy   210
lodging, sweetheart, thy lodging, or I'm a dead man!

HELLENA

Why must we be either guilty of fornication or murder
if we converse with you men? And is there no difference
between leave to love me, and leave to lie with me?

WILLMORE

Faith, child, they were made to go together.   215

LUCETTA (*pointing to* BLUNT)

Are you sure this is the man?

SANCHO

When did I mistake your game?

---

191 *Father Captain* alluding to Willmore's mock-adoption of a religious argument
193 *orders* final vows to make her a nun
206 *anything; I* ed. (anything, I Q1)
210 *swinging* fine, splendid
216 This is the first of several switches in focus on stage which occur throughout this
     scene.
217 *game* prey

LUCETTA

This is a stranger, I know by his gazing; if he be brisk
he'll venture to follow me, and then, if I understand my
trade, he's mine. He's English too, and they say that's a   220
sort of good-natured loving people, and have generally
so kind an opinion of themselves that a woman with any
wit may flatter 'em into any sort of fool she pleases.

She often passes by BLUNT *and gazes on him; he struts and*
cocks, and walks and gazes on her

BLUNT

'Tis so, she is taken – I have beauties which my false
glass at home did not discover.   225

FLORINDA (*Aside*)

This woman watches me so, I shall get no opportunity
to discover myself to him, and so miss the intent of my
coming. [*To* BELVILE] (*looking in his hand*) – But as I was
saying, sir – by this line you should be a lover.

BELVILE

I thought how right you guessed: all men are in love, or   230
pretend to be so. Come, let me go; I'm weary of this
fooling.

Walks away

FLORINDA

I will not till you have confessed whether the passion
that you have vowed Florinda be true or false.

She holds him; he strives to get from her

BELVILE (*turns quick towards her*)
Florinda!   235

FLORINDA
Softly.

BELVILE
Thou hast named one will fix me here forever.

FLORINDA
She'll be disappointed then, who expects you this night
at the garden gate. And if you fail not, as – (*looks on*
CALLIS, *who observes 'em*) let me see the other hand – you 240
will go near to do, she vows to die or make you happy.

BELVILE
What canst thou mean?

225 *glass* looking-glass
227 *discover* reveal
239–40 *looks . . . 'em* s.d. follows speech Q1

FLORINDA

That which I say. Farewell.

Offers to go

BELVILE

Oh charming sybil, stay; complete that joy which as it is
will turn into distraction! Where must I be? At the   245
garden gate? I know it. At night, you say? I'll sooner
forfeit Heaven than disobey.

Enter DON PEDRO *and other maskers, and
pass over the stage*

CALLIS

Madam, your brother's here.

FLORINDA

Take this to instruct you farther.

Gives him a letter, and goes off

FREDERICK

Have a care, sir, what you promise; this may be a trap   250
laid by her brother to ruin you. – *not as naïve as the others*

BELVILE

Do not disturb my happiness with doubts.

Opens the letter

WILLMORE [*To* HELLENA]

My dear pretty creature, a thousand blessings on thee!
Still in this habit, you say? And after dinner at this place?

HELLENA

Yes, if you will swear to keep your heart and not bestow   255
it between this and that. – *testing him – looking for something*

WILLMORE   *more permanent than a one night stand*

By all the little gods of love, I swear; I'll leave it with
you, and if you run away with it, those deities of justice
will revenge me.

Exeunt all the women [except LUCETTA]

FREDERICK

Do you know the hand?   260

BELVILE

'Tis Florinda's.

All blessings fall upon the virtuous maid.

FREDERICK

Nay, no idolatry; a sober sacrifice I'll allow you.

BELVILE

Oh friends, the welcom'st news! The softest letter! –

254 *habit* outfit

Nay, you shall all see it! And could you now be serious,   265
I might be made the happiest man the sun shines on!

WILLMORE

The reason of this mighty joy?

BELVILE

See how kindly she invites me to deliver her from the
threatened violence of her brother. Will you not assist
me?   270

WILLMORE

I know not what thou mean'st, but I'll make one at
any mischief where a woman's concerned. But she'll be
grateful to us for the favour, will she not?

BELVILE

How mean you?

WILLMORE

How should I mean? Thou know'st there's but one way   275
for a woman to oblige me.

BELVILE

Do not profane – the maid is nicely virtuous.

WILLMORE

Who, pox, then she's fit for nothing but a husband. Let
her e'en go, colonel.

FREDERICK

Peace, she's the colonel's mistress, sir.   280

WILLMORE

Let her be the devil; if she be thy mistress, I'll serve her.
Name the way.

BELVILE

Read here this postscript.

Gives him a letter

WILLMORE (*reads*)

'At ten at night – at the garden gate, of which, if I cannot
get the key, I will contrive a way over the wall – come   285
attended with a friend or two.' – Kind heart, if we three
cannot weave a string to let her down a garden wall,
'twere pity but the hangman wove one for us all.

FREDERICK

Let her alone for that; your woman's wit, your fair kind
woman, will out-trick a broker or a Jew, and contrive   290
like a Jesuit in chains. – But see, Ned Blunt is stolen out
after the lure of a damsel.

Exeunt BLUNT *and* LUCETTA

277 *nicely* scrupulously
290–1 *a broker … chains* All were associated with shrewd bargaining or persuasive
    argument.

BELVILE

So, he'll scarce find his way home again unless we get
him cried by the bellman in the market place. And
'twould sound prettily – a lost English boy of thirty.   295

FREDERICK

I hope 'tis some common crafty sinner, one that will fit
him. It may be she'll sell him for Peru: the rogue's sturdy,
and would work well in a mine. At least I hope she'll
dress him for our mirth, cheat him of all, then have him
well-favouredly banged, and turned out naked at   300
midnight.

WILLMORE

Prithee what humour is he of, that you wish him so well?

BELVILE

Why, of an English elder brother's humour: educated in
a nursery, with a maid to tend him till fifteen, and lies
with his grandmother till he's of age; one that knows no   305
pleasure beyond riding to the next fair, or going up to
London with his right worshipful father in parliament
time, wearing gay clothes, or making honourable love to
his lady mother's laundry maid; gets drunk at a hunting
match, and ten to one then gives some proofs of his   310
prowess. – A pox upon him, he's our banker, and has all
our cash about him; and if he fail, we are all broke.

FREDERICK

Oh, let him alone for that matter; he's of a damned
stingy quality, that will secure our stock. I know not in
what danger it were indeed if the jilt should pretend   315
she's in love with him, for 'tis a kind believing coxcomb;
otherwise, if he part with more than a piece of eight –
geld him: for which offer he may chance to be beaten if
she be a whore of the first rank.

BELVILE

Nay, the rogue will not be easily beaten; he's stout   320
enough. Perhaps if they talk beyond his capacity he may
chance to exercise his courage upon some of them, else
I'm sure they'll find it as difficult to beat as to please
him.

294 *cried by the bellman* cried out for by the town crier
297 *for Peru* as a slave in the mines of Peru
300 *banged* beaten violently
311 *banker* the one elected to look after all their funds
314 *stock* fund, i.e. sum of money set apart to provide for certain expenses
315 *jilt* wench, prostitute
317 *piece of eight* the old Spanish dollar

WILLMORE

'Tis a lucky devil to light upon so kind a wench!   325

FREDERICK

Thou hadst a great deal of talk with thy little gipsy;
couldst thou do no good upon her? For mine was hard-
hearted.

WILLMORE

Hang her, she was some damned honest person of
quality, I'm sure; she was so very free and witty. If her 330
face be but answerable to her wit and humour, I would
be bound to constancy this month to gain her. In the
meantime, have you made no kind acquaintance since
you came to town? You do not use to be honest so long,
gentlemen.   335

FREDERICK

Faith, love has kept us honest; we have been all fired
with a beauty newly come to town, the famous Paduana
Angellica Bianca.

WILLMORE

What, the mistress of the dead Spanish general?

BELVILE

Yes, she's now the only adored beauty of all the youth 340
in Naples, who put on all their charms to appear lovely
in her sight – their coaches, liveries, and themselves all
gay as on a monarch's birthday to attract the eyes of this
fair charmer, while she has the pleasure to behold all
languish for her that see her.   345

FREDERICK

'Tis pretty to see with how much love the men regard
her, and how much envy the women.

WILLMORE

What gallant has she?

BELVILE

None; she's exposed to sale, and four days in the week
she's yours – for so much a month.   350

WILLMORE

The very thought of it quenches all manner of fire in
me. Yet prithee, let's see her.   *wants instant satisfaction rather than
                                    commitment*

329 *honest* chaste
330 *quality* 1) high rank in society 2) wealth
        free 1) noble 2) unrestrained
333 *made ... acquaintance* met no willing women
337 *Paduana* native of Padua
342 *liveries* servants' uniforms
348 *gallant* male champion
349 *sale* ed. (sail Q1)

BELVILE

Let's first to dinner, and after that we'll pass the day as
you please. But at night ye must all be at my devotion.

WILLMORE

I will not fail you.   355

[*Exeunt*]

Act II, Scene i

The long street
Enter BELVILE *and* FREDERICK *in masking habits, and* WILLMORE
in his own clothes, with a vizard in his hand

WILLMORE

But why thus disguised and muzzled?

BELVILE

Because whatever extravagances we commit in these
faces, our own may not be obliged to answer 'em.

WILLMORE

I should have changed my eternal buff, too; but no
matter, my little gipsy would not have found me out   5
then. For if she should change hers, it is impossible I
should know her unless I should hear her prattle. A pox
on't, I cannot get her out of my head. Pray Heaven, if
ever I do see her again, she prove damnably ugly, that I
may fortify myself against her tongue. — shatters but he would still have a power over him

BELVILE

Have a care of love, for o' my conscience she was not of
a quality to give thee any hopes.

WILLMORE

Pox on 'em, why do they draw a man in then? She has
played with my heart so, that 'twill never lie still till I
have met with some kind wench that will play the game   15
out with me. Oh, for my arms full of soft, white, kind –
woman! Such as I fancy Angellica.

BELVILE

This is her house, if you were but in stock to get

---

354 *at my devotion* dedicated to my sacred purpose, i.e. the rescue of Florinda
  0 s.d. 2 *masking habits* See I.i.61 s.d. note.
    s.d. 3 *vizard* face mask
  1 *muzzled* 1) masked 2) fitted with a restricting contraption over the mouth
  3 *faces* i.e. masks
  4 *buff* leather military coat
  18 *in stock* in funds, i.e. with financial means

admittance. They have not dined yet; I perceive the
picture is not out.   20

Enter BLUNT

WILLMORE

I long to see the shadow of the fair substance; a man
may gaze on that for nothing.

BLUNT

Colonel, thy hand. – And thine, Fred. I have been an
ass, a deluded fool, a very coxcomb from my birth till
this hour, and heartily repent my little faith.   25

BELVILE

What the devil's the matter with thee, Ned?

[BLUNT]

Oh, such a mistress.

FREDERICK

Such a girl!

WILLMORE

Ha! Where?

FREDERICK

Ay, where?   30

[BLUNT]

So fond, so amorous, so toying, and so fine! And all for
sheer love, ye rogue! Oh, how she looked and kissed!
And soothed my heart from my bosom! I cannot think
I was awake, and yet methinks I see and feel her charms
still. – Fred, try if she have not left the taste of her balmy   35
kisses upon my lips –

Kisses him

BELVILE

Ha! Ha! Ha!

WILLMORE

Death, man, where is she?

19–20 *the picture* i.e. of Angellica
23 *Colonel* ed. (Coll. Q1)
24 *coxcomb* See I.i.123 note.
27–30 lineation ed. (– Oh such a Mrs. *Fred.* such a Girl! / *Will.* Ha! where. *Fred.* Ay
  where! Q1)
27 s.p. BLUNT Q3 (om. Q1, Q2, C) The indented dash before 'Oh such' in Q1
  suggests that a speech prefix is missing, and Blunt is the obvious candidate as
  Belvile has just addressed him.
28 and 30 In Q1 Frederick's s.p. and speech run on with ll. 27 and 29 respectively.
31 s.p. BLUNT Q3, C (om. Q1, Q2). In Q1 the speech, which is characteristic of
  Blunt, is indented, as if a speech prefix is missing.
38 lineation Q3 (s.p. and speech run on with l. 37 Q1, Q2, C)

[BLUNT]

What a dog was I to stay in dull England so long! How
have I laughed at the colonel when he sighed for love!   40
But now the little archer has revenged him! And by this
one dart I can guess at all his joys, which then I took for
fancies, mere dreams and fables. Well, I'm resolved to
sell all in Essex and plant here forever.

BELVILE

What a blessing 'tis, thou hast a mistress thou dar'st   45
boast of; for I know thy humour is rather to have a
proclaimed clap than a secret amour.

WILLMORE

Dost know her name?

BLUNT

Her name? No, 'sheartlikins. What care I for names?
She's fair, young, brisk and kind, even to ravishment!   50
And what a pox care I for knowing her by any other
title?

WILLMORE

Didst give her anything?

BLUNT

Give her! Ha! Ha! Ha! Why, she's a person of quality. –
That's a good one! Give her! 'Sheartlikins, dost think   55
such creatures are to be bought? Or are we provided for
such a purchase? Give her, quoth ye? Why, she presented
me with this bracelet for the toy of a diamond I used to
wear. No, gentlemen, Ned Blunt is not everybody. She
expects me again tonight.   60

WILLMORE

Egad, that's well; we'll all go.

BLUNT

Not a soul! No, gentlemen, you are wits; I am a dull
country rogue, I.

FREDERICK

Well, sir, for all your person of quality, I shall be very
glad to understand your purse be secure; 'tis our whole   65

---

39 s.p. BLUNT Q3, C (om. Q1, Q2) As at l. 27, an indented dash in Q1 suggests a
   missing speech prefix, and the reference to 'Essex' at l. 44 identifies Blunt as the
   speaker.
41 *little archer* Cupid
44 *all in Essex* all his lands at home
47 *proclaimed clap* apparent signs of gonorrhoea
54 *quality* See I.ii. 330 note.
61 *Egad* by God!

estate at present, which we are loath to hazard in one
bottom. Come sir, unlade.

BLUNT

Take the necessary trifle useless now to me, that am
beloved by such a gentlewoman. 'Sheartlikins, money!
Here, take mine too.   70

FREDERICK

No, keep that to be cozened, that we may laugh.

WILLMORE

Cozened? Death! Would I could meet with one that
would cozen me of all the love I could spare tonight.

FREDERICK

Pox, 'tis some common whore, upon my life.

BLUNT

A whore? Yes, with such clothes, such jewels, such a   75
house, such furniture, and so attended! A whore!

BELVILE

Why yes, sir, they are whores, though they'll neither
entertain you with drinking, swearing, or bawdry; are
whores in all those gay clothes and right jewels; are
whores with those great houses richly furnished with   80
velvet beds, store of plate, handsome attendance, and
fine coaches; are whores, and arrant ones.

WILLMORE

Pox on't, where do these fine whores live?

BELVILE

Where no rogues in office, ecliped constables, dare give
'em laws, nor the wine-inspired bullies of the town break 85
their windows; yet they are whores though this Essex
calf believe 'em persons of quality.

BLUNT

'Sheartlikins, y'are all fools. There are things about this
Essex calf that shall take with the ladies, beyond all your
wit and parts. This shape and size, gentlemen, are not   90
to be despised; my waist, too, tolerably long, with other
inviting signs that shall be nameless.

---

67 *bottom* ship, vessel
    unlade take the cargo out
71 *cozened* cheated
73 *cozen* beguile
79 *right* genuine
81 *plate* i.e. silver or gold-plated ware
82 *arrant* (errant Q1) unmitigated, thorough
84 *ecliped* known as
86–7 *Essex calf* foolish fellow

WILLMORE

Egad, I believe he may have met with some person of
quality that may be kind to him.

BELVILE

Dost thou perceive any such tempting things about him   95
that should make a fine woman, and of quality, pick him
out from all mankind to throw away her youth and
beauty upon; nay, and her dear heart, too? No, no,
Angellica has raised the price too high.

WILLMORE

May she languish for mankind till she die, and be   100
damned for that one sin alone.

*Enter two bravos and hang up a great picture of Angellica
against the balcony, and two little ones at each side of the
door* [*stating her terms*]

BELVILE

See there, the fair sign to the inn where a man may lodge
that's fool enough to give her price.

WILLMORE *gazes on the picture*

BLUNT

'Sheartlikins, gentlemen, what's this?

BELVILE

A famous courtesan, that's to be sold.   105

BLUNT

How? To be sold? Nay, then I have nothing to say to
her. Sold? What impudence is practised in this country?
With what order and decency whoring's established here
by virtue of the Inquisition! Come, let's be gone; I'm
sure we're no chapmen for this commodity.   110

FREDERICK

Thou art none, I'm sure, unless thou couldst have her
in thy bed at a price of a coach in the street.

99 *the price* i.e. of women's sexual favours
100 *languish* waste away with desire for
101 s.d. 1 *bravos* See I.ii.129 note.
    Angellica ed. (Angellica's Q1)
105 *courtesan* euphemism for prostitute
109 *the Inquisition* an ironic reference to a later form of the Roman Catholic medieval
    institution, authorised by Pope Sixtus IV in 1478 to combat heresy, witchcraft,
    and sorcery
110 *chapmen* purchasers, customers

WILLMORE

How wondrous fair she is. A thousand crowns a month?
By Heaven, as many kingdoms were too little! A plague
of this poverty, of which I ne'er complain but when it   115
hinders my approach to beauty, which virtue ne'er could
purchase.   *Turns from the picture*

BLUNT

What's this? – (*Reads*) 'A thousand crowns a month'!
'Sheartlikins, here's a sum! Sure 'tis a mistake. [*To one
of the bravos*] – Hark you, friend, does she take or give   120
so much by the month?

FREDERICK

A thousand crowns! Why, 'tis a portion for the Infanta.

BLUNT

Hark ye, friends, won't she trust?

BRAVO

This is a trade, sir, that cannot live by credit.

Enter DON PEDRO *in masquerade, followed by* STEPHANO

BELVILE

See, here's more company; let's walk off a while.   125
                         Exeunt English [BELVILE, FREDERICK,
                              WILLMORE, *and* BLUNT]

PEDRO *reads*

PEDRO

Fetch me a thousand crowns; I never wished to buy this
beauty at an easier rate.

                         Passes off [*with* STEPHANO]

Enter ANGELLICA *and* MORETTA *in the balcony,
and draw a silk curtain*

ANGELLICA [*To the bravo*]

Prithee, what said those fellows to thee?

BRAVO

Madam, the first were admirers of beauty only, but no
purchasers; they were merry with your price and picture,   130
laughed at the sum, and so passed off.

ANGELLICA

No matter, I'm not displeased with their rallying; their

---

113 *a thousand crowns* A crown was 5 shillings (25p), so Angellica charged £250 a
      month – a large amount in the 1650s.

122 *portion ... the Infanta* dowry ... the daughter of the Spanish sovereign

127 s.d. 3 *draw ... curtain* presumably near the front of the balcony area (see l. 198
      s.d.)

132 *rallying* bantering, good-humoured ridicule

detached
sees love
as a business
transaction

wonder feeds my vanity, and he that wishes but to buy
gives me more pride than he that gives my price can
make my pleasure.   135

BRAVO
Madam, the last I knew through all his disguises to be
Don Pedro, nephew to the general, and who was with
him in Pamplona.

ANGELICA
Don Pedro? My old gallant's nephew! When his uncle
died he left him a vast sum of money; it is he who was   140
so in love with me at Padua, and who used to make the
general so jealous.

MORETTA
Is this he that used to prance before our window, and
take such care to show himself an amorous ass? If I am
not mistaken, he is the likeliest man to give your price.   145

ANGELICA

knows that
men cannot
give her anything
money
better?

The man is brave and generous, but of an humour so
uneasy and inconstant that the victory over his heart is
as soon lost as won; a slave that can add little to the
triumph of the conqueror. But inconstancy's the sin of
all mankind, therefore I'm resolved that nothing but   150
gold shall charm my heart.

MORETTA
I'm glad on't; 'tis only interest that women of our profession ought to consider, though I wonder what has
kept you from that general disease of our sex so long; I
mean that of being in love.   155

ANGELICA

never will
fall in love
would destroy
us.

A kind but sullen star under which I had the happiness
to be born. Yet I have had no time for love; the bravest
and noblest of mankind have purchased my favours at
so dear a rate, as if no coin but gold were current with
our trade. – But here's Don Pedro again; fetch me my   160
lute – for 'tis for him or Don Antonio, the viceroy's son,
that I have spread my nets.

Enter at one door DON PEDRO [*and*] STEPHANO; DON
ANTONIO *and* DIEGO [*his page*] *at the other door, with
people following him in masquerade, anticly attired, some
with music. They both go up to the picture*

---

138 *Pamplona* ed. (Pampalona Q1) See I.i.55 note.
139 *gallant* See I.ii.348 note.
162 s.d. 3 *anticly* bizarrely

ANTONIO

A thousand crowns! Had not the painter flattered her, I
should not think it dear.

PEDRO

Flattered her? By Heaven, he cannot. I have seen the   165
original, nor is there one charm here more than adorns
her face and eyes; all this soft and sweet, with a certain
languishing air that no artist can represent.

ANTONIO

What I heard of her beauty before had fired my soul,
but this confirmation of it has blown it to a flame.   170

PEDRO

Ha!

PAGE

Sir, I have known you throw away a thousand crowns
on a worse face, and though y'are near your marriage,
you may venture a little love here; Florinda will not miss
it.   175

PEDRO (*Aside*)

Ha! Florinda! Sure 'tis Antonio.

ANTONIO

Florinda! Name not those distant joys; there's not one
thought of her will check my passion here.

PEDRO (*Aside*)

shocked — Florinda scorned! (*A noise of a lute above*) And all my
& double hopes defeated of the possession of Angellica! (*Antonio* 180
standard *gazes up*) Her injuries, by Heaven, he shall not boast of!
perhaps when it concerns his sister?

Song to a lute above

SONG

[I]

When Damon first began to love
      He languished in a soft desire,
And knew not how the gods to move,
      To lessen or increase his fire.   185
For Caelia in her charming eyes
Wore all love's sweets, and all his cruelties.

II

But as beneath a shade he lay,
Weaving of flowers for Caelia's hair,
She chanced to lead her flock that way,   190

182 *Damon* Virgil's shepherd singer (eighth Eclogue): in poetry the name signified a
     rustic swain.
186 *Caelia* The name means 'heavenly'.

And saw the am'rous shepherd there.
She gazed around upon the place,
And saw the grove, resembling night,
To all the joys of love invite,
Whilst guilty smiles and blushes dressed her face.   195
At this the bashful youth all transport grew,
And with kind force he taught the virgin how
To yield what all his sighs could never do.

ANGELLICA *throws open the curtains and bows to* ANTONIO,
who pulls off his vizard and bows and blows up kisses.
PEDRO, *unseen, looks in's face*

ANTONIO
By Heaven, she's charming fair!
PEDRO (*Aside*)
'Tis he, the false Antonio! — breaking up of friendship   200
                              is realises that he is not the
ANTONIO (*To the bravo*)   best match for
Friend, where must I pay my off'ring of love?   florinda?
My thousand crowns I mean.
PEDRO
That off'ring I have designed to make,
And yours will come too late.
ANTONIO
Prithee begone; I shall grow angry else,   205
And then thou art not safe.
PEDRO
My anger may be fatal, sir, as yours,
And he that enters here may prove this truth.
ANTONIO
I know not who thou art, but I am sure thou'rt worth
my killing, for aiming at Angellica. — passionate over   210
                                        love
They draw and fight
Enter WILLMORE *and* BLUNT, *who draw and part 'em*

BLUNT
'Sheartlikins, here's fine doings.
WILLMORE
Tilting for the wench, I'm sure. Nay, gad, if that would
win her I have as good a sword as the best of ye. – Put
up, put up, and take another time and place, for this is
designed for lovers only.   215

They all put up

198 s.d. Q1, Q2 (follows l. 200 Q3, C)
212 *tilting* combating as in duelling
213–14 *put up* put away, i.e. your swords

PEDRO

    We are prevented; dare you meet me tomorrow on the
    Molo?
    For I've a title to a better quarrel,
    That of Florinda, in whose credulous heart
    Thou'st made an int'rest, and destroyed my hopes.   220

ANTONIO

    Dare!
    I'll meet thee there as early as the day.

PEDRO

    We will come thus disguised, that whosoever chance to
    get the better, he may escape unknown.

ANTONIO

    It shall be so.   225

                  Exeunt PEDRO *and* STEPHANO
    Who should this rival be? Unless the English colonel, of
    whom I've often heard Don Pedro speak; it must be he,
    and time he were removed, who lays a claim to all my
    happiness.

        WILLMORE *having gazed all this while on the picture,*
                pulls down a little one

WILLMORE

    This posture's loose and negligent,   230
    The sight on't would beget a warm desire
    In souls whom impotence and age had chilled.
    This must along with me.

BRAVO

    What means this rudeness, sir? Restore the picture.

ANTONIO

    Ha! Rudeness committed to the fair Angellica! – Restore 235
    the picture, sir.

WILLMORE

    Indeed I will not, sir.

ANTONIO

    By Heaven but you shall.

WILLMORE

    Nay, do not show your sword; if you do, by this dear
    beauty – I will show mine too.   240

ANTONIO

    What right can you pretend to't?

217 *Molo* mall
231 *beget* generate
234 *Restore* replace

WILLMORE

That of possession which I will maintain. You, perhaps,
have a 1000 crowns to give for the original.

ANTONIO

No matter, sir, you shall restore the picture.

ANGELLICA and MORETTA [*appear*] *above*

ANGELLICA

Oh Moretta! What's the matter?   245

ANTONIO [*To* WILLMORE]

Or leave your life behind.

WILLMORE

Death! You lie – I will do neither.

They fight. The Spaniards join with ANTONIO,
BLUNT *laying on like mad*

ANGELLICA

Hold, I command you, if for me you fight.

They leave off and bow

WILLMORE

How heavenly fair she is! Ah plague of her price.

ANGELLICA

You, sir, in buff; you that appear a soldier, that first 250
began this insolence –

WILLMORE

'Tis true, I did so, if you call it insolence for a man to
preserve himself. I saw your charming picture and was
wounded; quite through my soul each pointed beauty
ran; and wanting a thousand crowns to procure my   255
remedy – I laid this little picture to my bosom – which
if you cannot allow me, I'll resign.

ANGELLICA

No, you may keep the trifle.

ANTONIO

You shall first ask me leave, and this.

[They] fight again as before
Enter BELVILE *and* FREDERICK *who join*
with the English [BLUNT *and* WILLMORE]

244 s.d. Q2 (s.d. follows l. 245 Q1, Q3, C)
247 s.d. ed. (after l. 248 Q1–3, C)
250 *buff* leather
255 *wanting* lacking
257 *resign* relinquish

ANGELICA

Hold! Will you ruin me! – Biskey – Sebastian! – Part   260
'em!

The Spaniards are beaten off

MORETTA

drama raises another putting them out of a job Oh madam, we're undone! A pox upon that rude fellow, he's set on to ruin us: we shall never see good days till all these fighting poor rogues are sent to the galleys.

Enter BELVILE, BLUNT, FREDERICK, *and* WILLMORE *with's shirt bloody*

BLUNT

'Sheartlikins, beat me at this sport, and I'll ne'er wear   265
sword more.

BELVILE (*To* WILLMORE)

The devil's in thee for a mad fellow, thou art always one
at an unlucky adventure – come let's begone whilst we're
safe, and remember these are Spaniards, a sort of people
that know how to revenge an affront.   270

FREDERICK

You bleed! I hope you are not wounded.

WILLMORE

Not much. A plague on your Dons; if they fight no better
they'll ne'er recover Flanders. – What the devil was't to
them that I took down the picture?

BLUNT

Took it! 'Sheartlikins we'll have the great one too; 'tis   275
ours by conquest. – Prithee help me up and I'll pull it
down –

ANGELICA

Stay sir, and ere you affront me farther, let me know
how you durst commit this outrage – to you I speak sir,
for you appear a gentleman.   280

WILLMORE

To me, madam? – Gentlemen, your servant.

[*He is about to exit with* ANGELICA;] BELVILE *stays him*

BELVILE

Is the devil in thee? Dost know the danger of ent'ring
the house of an incensed courtesan?

irony in that it is AB who is in danger rather than Willmore.

261 s.d. *The Spaniards ... off* Belvile, Blunt, Frederick, and Willmore exit, driving
Antonio, Diego, and the bravos, Biskey and Sebastian, off-stage.
264 *the galleys* low flat-built vessels rowed by condemned criminals or slaves
272 *Dons* Spaniards
273 *they'll ne'er recover Flanders* In the late seventeenth century a large section of
Flanders became French territory.

WILLMORE

I thank you for your care – but there are other matters
in hand, there are, though we have no great temptation. –   285
Death! Let me go!

FREDERICK

Yes, to your lodging if you will, but not in here. – Damn
these gay harlots. – By this hand I'll have as sound and
handsome a whore for a patacoon. – Death, man, she'll
murder thee. *aware of the dangers*   290

WILLMORE

Oh, fear me not! Shall I not venture where a beauty *reckless and*
calls? A lovely charming beauty! For fear of danger! *blind to his*
When, by Heaven, there's none so great as to long for *friends warning*
her, whilst I want money to purchase her.

[FREDERICK]

Therefore 'tis loss of time unless you had the thousand   295
crowns to pay.

WILLMORE

It may be she may give a favour; at least I shall have the
pleasure of saluting her when I enter, and when I depart.

BELVILE

Pox, she'll as soon lie with thee as kiss thee, and sooner
stab than do either. – You shall not go.   300

ANGELLICA

Fear not, sir; all I have to wound with is my eyes.

BLUNT [*To* BELVILE]

Let him go. 'Sheartlikins, I believe the gentlewoman
means well.

BELVILE

Well, take thy fortune; we'll expect you in the next street.
Farewell, fool. Farewell.   305

WILLMORE

Bye, colonel.   *Goes in*

FREDERICK

The rogue's stark mad for a wench.

                                                 Exeunt

285–300 The dashes in Q1 could be meant to indicate that a physical struggle is
    taking place.

289 *patacoon* a Portuguese and Spanish silver coin worth about 24p

295 s.p. FREDERICK Q3 (PEDRO Q1, Q2, C) Q3's emendation is necessary as Pedro
    left the stage at l. 225.

301 *all . . . eyes* alluding to a Petrarchan conceit popular in sixteenth and seventeenth-
    century love poetry, in which the rejected lover claimed to have been slain by a
    cruel glance

[Act II,] Scene [ii]

A fine chamber
Enter WILLMORE, ANGELLICA, *and* MORETTA

ANGELLICA
Insolent sir, how durst you pull down my picture?

[margin note: On control plans to use his wit over her.]

WILLMORE
Rather, how durst you set it up to tempt poor am'rous
mortals with so much excellence, which I find you have
but too well consulted by the unmerciful price you set   5
upon't. Is all this heaven of beauty shown to move
despair in those that cannot buy? And can you think
th'effects of that despair should be less extravagant than
I have shown?

[margin note: remains professional]

ANGELLICA
I sent for you to ask my pardon, sir, not to aggravate
your crime. I thought I should have seen you at my feet   10
imploring it.

WILLMORE
You are deceived. I came to rail at you, and rail such
truths, too, as shall let you see the vanity of that pride
which taught you how to set such price on sin.
For such it is, whilst that which is love's due   15
is meanly bartered for.   *[margin note: speaks of love – AB has no concept of it.]*

ANGELLICA
Ha! ha! ha! Alas, good captain, what pity 'tis your edi-
fying doctrine will do no good upon me. – Moretta!
Fetch the gentleman a glass, and let him survey himself.
To see what charms he has (*aside, in a soft tone*) – and   20
guess my business. *[margin note: does not easily submit to his power.]*

MORETTA
He knows himself of old; I believe those breeches and
he have been acquainted ever since he was beaten at
Worcester.

ANGELLICA
Nay, do not abuse the poor creature –   25

MORETTA
[margin note: does not fall for Willmore's words]
Good weather-beaten corporal, will you march off? We
have no need of your doctrine, though you have of our
charity. But at present we have no scraps; we can afford

[margin note: still focused on money, illuminates AB's flaws]

0 s.d. 1 See I.i.0 s.d. 1 note.
19 *glass* See I.ii.225 note.
22 *breeches* trousers which reach just below the knee
24 *Worcester* On 3 September 1651 Cromwell finally defeated Charles II at Worcester
and ended the Civil War.

no kindness for God's sake; in fine, sirrah, the price is
too high i'th' mouth for you, therefore troop, I say.   30
WILLMORE [*To* MORETTA]
Here, good forewoman of the shop, serve me, and I'll
be gone.

[Offers her money]

MORETTA
Keep it to pay your laundress, your linen stinks of the
gun room – for here's no selling by retail.
WILLMORE
Thou hast sold plenty of thy stale ware at a cheap rate.   35
MORETTA
Ay, the more silly kind heart I; but this is an age wherein
beauty is at higher rates. In fine, you know the price of
this.
WILLMORE
I grant you 'tis here set down, a thousand crowns a
month. Pray, how much may come to my share for a   40
pistole? Bawd, take your black-lead and sum it up, that
I may have a pistole's worth of this vain gay thing, and
I'll trouble you no more.
MORETTA
Pox on him, he'll fret me to death. – Abominable fellow,
I tell thee, we only sell by the whole piece.   45
WILLMORE
'Tis very hard, the whole cargo or nothing. Faith,
madam, my stock will not reach it; I cannot be your
chapman. Yet I have countrymen in town, merchants of
love like me; I'll see if they'll put in for a share. We
cannot lose much by it, and what we have no use for,   50
we'll sell upon the Friday's mart at 'Who gives more?' I
am studying, madam, how to purchase you, though at
present I am unprovided of money.
ANGELLICA [*Aside*]
Sure, this from any other man would anger me – nor

– first sign of her weakness.

30 *high i'th' mouth* To 'open one's mouth wide' meant to ask a high price.
     troop be off
31 *forewoman* manageress
39 *here* i.e. on the picture he's holding
41 *pistole* a Spanish gold coin worth between 82.5 and 90p
     black-lead pencil
42 *thing* Q3 (things Q1, Q2, C)
47 *stock* funds
48 *chapman* purchaser
51 *mart . . . more* auction

shall he know the conquest he has made. – Poor angry   55
man, how I despise this railing.

WILLMORE
Yes, I am poor – but I'm a gentleman,
And one that scorns this baseness which you practise.
Poor as I am, I would not sell myself.
No, not to gain your charming high prized person.   60
Though I admire you strangely for your beauty,
Yet I condemn your mind.
And yet I would at any rate enjoy you;
At your own rate – but cannot. – See here
The only sum I can command on earth;   65
I know not where to eat when this is gone.
Yet such a slave I am to love and beauty
This last reserve I'll sacrifice to enjoy you.
Nay, do not frown; I know you're to be bought,
And would be bought by me. By me,   70
For a mean trifling sum if I could pay it down.
Which happy knowledge I will still repeat,
And lay it to my heart: it has a virtue in't,
And soon will cure those wounds your eyes have made.
And yet – there's something so divinely powerful there –   75
Nay, I will gaze – to let you see my strength.

Holds her, looks on her, and pauses and sighs

By Heaven, bright creature, I would not for the world
Thy fame were half so fair as is thy face.

Turns her away from him

ANGELLICA [*Aside*]
His words go through me to the very soul.
[*To him*] – If you have nothing else to say to me –   80
WILLMORE
Yes, you shall hear how infamous you are –
For which I do not hate thee –
But that secures my heart, and all the flames it feels
Are but so many lusts;
I know it by their sudden bold intrusion.   85
The fire's impatient and betrays; 'tis false –
For had it been the purer flame of love,
I should have pined and languished at your feet,

63 *enjoy you* possess your body for my pleasure
74 *cure* Q1, Q3 (curse Q2, C)
    wounds . . . eyes See II.i.301 note.
78 *fame* reputation

Ere found the impudence to have discovered it.
I now dare stand your scorn and your denial.   90

MORETTA [*Aside*]
Sure she's bewitched, that she can stand thus tamely *aware of*
and hear his saucy railing. – Sirrah, will you be gone? *ABs fall.*

ANGELLICA [*To* MORETTA]
How dare you take this liberty! Withdraw. [MORETTA
withdraws, but remains on-stage] – Pray tell me, sir, are
not you guilty of the same mercenary crime? When a   *makes a*   95
lady is proposed to you for a wife, you never ask how *mockery of the*
fair, discreet, or virtuous she is, but 'What's her for- *marriage*
tune?' – which, if but small, you cry, 'She will not do my *system*
business', and basely leave her, though she languish for *insight*   100
you. Say, is not this as poor?   *into her decision*

WILLMORE   *to be a*
It is a barbarous custom, which I will scorn to defend in *courtezan*
our sex, and do despise in yours. – *believes it is*
                                    mainly on the woman's
ANGELLICA   *part*
Thou'rt a brave fellow! Put up thy gold, and know,
That were thy fortune large as is thy soul,
Thou shouldst not buy my love   105
Couldst thou forget those mean effects of vanity
Which set me out to sale, and, as a lover,
Prize my yielding joys.
Canst thou believe they'll be entirely thine,
Without considering they were mercenary?   110

WILLMORE
I cannot tell; I must bethink me first – [*aside*] – ha!
Death, I'm going to believe her. – *realises way to her heart.*

ANGELLICA
Prithee, confirm that faith – or if thou canst not – flatter
me a little; 'twill please me from thy mouth. – *clever in her*
                                                 game.
WILLMORE (*Aside*)
Curse on thy charming tongue! Dost thou return   115
My feigned contempt with so much subtlety?
[*To her*] – Thou'st found the easiest way into my heart,
Though I yet know that all thou say'st is false.
                                       – pretends to be hurt
        Turning from her in rage   *↳ has a true*
                                                 heart.
ANGELLICA
By all that's good, 'tis real;
I never loved before, though oft a mistress.   120
– has never known love because she has always
shut down her emotions.

91 *bewitched* Q2, Q3, C (bewitch Q1)
99 *though* Q2, Q3, C (thou Q1)
107 *which . . . lover,* ed. (which . . . joys. one line in Q1)

Shall my first vows be slighted?
WILLMORE (*Aside*)
What can she mean?
ANGELLICA (*in an angry tone*)
I find you cannot credit me.
WILLMORE
I know you take me for an arrant ass,
An ass that may be soothed into belief,   125
And then be used at pleasure;
But, madam, I have been so often cheated
By perjured, soft, deluding hypocrites,
That I've no faith left for the cozening sex,
Especially for women of your trade.   130
ANGELLICA
The low esteem you have of me, perhaps
May bring my heart again:
For I have pride, that yet surmounts my love.

          She turns with pride: he holds her

WILLMORE
Throw off this pride, this enemy to bliss,
And show the power of love: 'tis with those arms   135
I can be only vanquished, made a slave.
ANGELLICA
Is all my mighty expectation vanished?
No, I will not hear thee talk; thou hast a charm
In every word that draws my heart away.
And all the thousand trophies I designed   140
Thou hast undone. Why art thou soft?
Thy looks are bravely rough, and meant for war.
Could'st thou not storm on still?
I then, perhaps, had been as free as thou.
WILLMORE (*Aside*)
Death, how she throws her fire about my soul!   145
[*To her*] – Take heed, fair creature, how you raise my
    hopes,
Which once assumed pretend to all dominion.
There's not a joy thou hast in store,
I shall not then command.
For which I'll pay thee back my soul, my life!   150
Come, let's begin th'account this happy minute!
ANGELLICA
And will you pay me then the price I ask?

133 s.d. *turns with pride:* ed. (turns: with pride Q1)
147 *pretend* ed. (pretends Q1)

WILLMORE

Oh, why dost thou draw me from an awful worship,
By showing thou art no divinity.
Conceal the fiend, and show me all the angel!   155
Keep me but ignorant, and I'll be devout
And pay my vows forever at this shrine.

Kneels and kisses her hand

ANGELLICA

The pay I mean is but thy love for mine.   *— still demands a price*
Can you give that?   *but her terms differ*
                                             — wants assurance
WILLMORE   *— false?*

Entirely. Come, let's withdraw where I'll renew my   160
vows – and breathe 'em with such ardour thou shalt not
doubt my zeal.

ANGELLICA

Thou hast a power too strong to be resisted.

Exeunt WILLMORE *and* ANGELLICA

MORETTA

Now my curse go with you! Is all our project fallen to
this? To love the only enemy to our trade? Nay, to love   165
such a shameroon, a very beggar; nay, a pirate beggar,
whose business is to rifle and be gone; a no-purchase,
no-pay tatterdemalion, and English picaroon – a rogue
that fights for daily drink, and takes a pride in being
loyally lousy? Oh, I could curse now, if I durst. This is   170
the fate of most whores.

Trophies, which from believing fops we win,
Are spoils to those who cozen us again.   [*Exit*]

Act III, Scene i

A street

Enter FLORINDA, VALERIA, HELLENA, *in antic different dresses from
what they were in before,* CALLIS *attending*

FLORINDA

I wonder what should make my brother in so ill a
humour? I hope he has not found out our ramble this

153 *awful* full of awe, reverential
166 *shameroon* shameful person
168 *tatterdemalion* ragamuffin, beggar
    picaroon pirate, brigand watching out to seize a prize
  0 s.d. 2 *antic* bizarre
  2 *ramble* See I.i.202 note.

HELLENA

No, if he had, we should have heard on't at both ears,
and have been mewed up this afternoon; which I would   5
not for the world should have happened. Hey, ho, I'm
as sad as a lover's lute.

VALERIA

Well, methinks we have learnt this trade of gipsies as
readily as if we had been bred upon the road to Loretta:
and yet I did so fumble, when I told the stranger his   10
fortune, that I was afraid I should have told my own and
yours by mistake. But, methinks Hellena has been very
serious ever since.

FLORINDA

I would give my garters she were in love, to be revenged
upon her for abusing me. – How is't, Hellena?   15

HELLENA

Ah, would I had never seen my mad monsieur – and yet
for all your laughing, I am not in love – and yet this
small acquaintance o' my conscience will never out of
my head.

VALERIA

Ha, ha, ha! I laugh to think how thou art fitted with a   20
lover, a fellow that I warrant loves every new face he
sees.

HELLENA

Hum, he has not kept his word with me here, and may
be taken up – that thought is not very pleasant to me.
What the deuce should this be now that I feel?   25

VALERIA

What is't like?

HELLENA

Nay, the Lord knows – but if I should be hanged I cannot
choose but be angry and afraid when I think that mad
fellow should be in love with anybody but me: what to
think of myself, I know not. Would I could meet with   30
some true damned gipsy that I might know my fortune.

VALERIA

Know it! Why there's nothing so easy. Thou wilt love
this wandering inconstant till thou find'st thyself hanged
about his neck, and then be as mad to get free again.

5 *mewed* shut
6–7 *I'm as* Q1–3 (I'm, C)
24 *taken up* i.e. occupied with a new woman
25 *deuce* devil

FLORINDA

Yes, Valeria, we shall see her bestride his baggage horse   35
and follow him to the campaign.

HELLENA

So, so, now you are provided for, there's no care taken
of poor me: but since you have set my heart a-wishing,
I am resolved to know for what. I will not die of the pip,
so I will not. – *determined – strong*.   40

FLORINDA

Art thou mad to talk so? Who will like thee well enough *Hellena is*
to have thee, that hears what a mad wench thou art? *to overpower*

HELLENA

will not Like me! I don't intend every he that likes me shall have
e won over me, but he that I like. I should have stayed in the nunnery
y anyone still if I had liked my Lady Abbess as well as she liked   45
me. No, I came thence not, as my wise brother imagines,
to take an eternal farewell of the world, but to love and
to be beloved; and I will be beloved, or I'll get one of
your men, so I will. – *sees men as her way out of*
the nunnery rather than a love.

VALERIA

Am I put into the number of lovers?   50

HELLENA

You? Why coz, I know thou'rt too good-natured to leave
us in any design: thou wouldst venture a cast though
thou camest off a loser, especially with such a gamester.
I observe your man, and your willing ear incline that
way; and if you are not a lover, 'tis an art soon learnt   55
(*sighs*) – that I find.

FLORINDA

I wonder how you learnt to love so easily. I had a
thousand charms to meet my eyes and ears e'er I could
yield, and 'twas the knowledge of Belvile's merit, not the
surprising person, took my soul. Thou art too rash, to   60
give a heart at first sight.

HELLENA

ellena Hang your considering lover! I never thought beyond
is not sup the fancy that 'twas a very pretty, idle, silly kind of
e romantic pleasure to pass one's time with: to write little, soft,
iew of nonsensical *billets*, and with great difficulty and danger,   65
love.

39 *pip* a humorous general term for an ailment (in this case, being loveless)
51 *coz* cousin (used fondly of relatives and close friends)
52 *design* scheme   *wouldst* ed. (wou't, Q1, Q2; would Q3; won't C)
    venture a cast risk a throw of the dice
53 *camest* ed. (comest Q1)
64–5 *soft . . . billets* billets-doux, love letters

receive answers in which I shall have my beauty praised,
my wit admired – though little or none – and have the
vanity and power to know I am desirable. Then I have
the more inclination that way because I am to be a nun,
and so shall not be suspected to have any such earthly   70
thoughts about me, but when I walk thus – and sigh
thus – they'll think my mind's upon my monastery, and
cry, 'How happy 'tis she's so resolved'. But not a word
of man.

FLORINDA

What a mad creature's this?   75

HELLENA

I'll warrant, if my brother hears either of you sigh, he
cries gravely: 'I fear you have the indiscretion to be in
love, but take heed of the honour of our house and your
own unspotted fame', and so he conjures on till he has
laid the soft winged god in your hearts, or broke the   80
bird's nest. – But see, here comes your lover, but where's
my inconstant? Let's step aside and we may learn something. *is continually refers to him as that*
         shows her perception.   [*They*] go aside

Enter BELVILE, FREDERICK, *and* BLUNT

BELVILE

What means this! The picture's taken in.

BLUNT

It may be the wench is good-natured and will be kind   85
gratis. Your friend's a proper handsome fellow.

BELVILE

I rather think she has cut his throat and is fled: I am
mad he should throw himself into dangers. Pox on't, I
shall want him, too, at night. Let's knock and ask for
him.   90

HELLENA

My heart goes a-pit, a-pat, for fear 'tis my man they talk
of.

73–4 *But . . . man.* separate line in Q1

73 *a* Q2, Q3, C (om. Q1)

80 *soft winged god* Cupid

80–1 *laid . . . nest* i.e. until his behaviour has strengthened your resolution to love or
has destroyed it

85–6 *be kind gratis* give her sexual favours free of charge

86 *proper* See I.i.42 note.

89 *too, at night* ed. (too at Night Q1, Q3; tonight Q2, C)
     want . . . night i.e. lack his help tonight (in Florinda's rescue)

[BELVILE *and* BLUNT] *knock*; MORETTA [*appears*] *above*

MORETTA
What would you have?

BELVILE
Tell the stranger that entered here about two hours ago
that his friends stay here for him.   95

MORETTA
A curse upon him for Moretta! Would he were at the
devil – but he's coming to you.

[*Enter* WILLMORE]

HELLENA
I, I, 'tis he! Oh, how this vexes me. — *feels herself unwittingly falling for him.*

BELVILE
And how, and how dear lad, has fortune smiled? Are we
to break her windows, or raise up altars to her, ha?   100

WILLMORE
Does not my fortune sit triumphant on my brow? Dost
not see the little wanton god there, all gay and smiling?
Have I not an air about my face and eyes that distinguish
me from the crowd of common lovers? By Heaven,
Cupid's quiver has not half so many darts as her eyes!   105
Oh, such a *bona roba*! To sleep in her arms is lying in
fresco, all perfumed air about me.

HELLENA (*Aside*)
Here's fine encouragement for me to fool on. — *returns to her scheming.*

WILLMORE
Hark'ee, where didst thou purchase that rich Canary we
drank today? Tell me, that I may adore the spigot and   110
sacrifice to the butt! The juice was divine – into which I
must dip my rosary, and then bless all things that I
would have bold or fortunate!

BELVILE
Well sir, let's go take a bottle and hear the story of your
success.   115

FREDERICK
Would not French wine do better?

---

95 *stay* wait
106 *bona roba* It. *buona* (good) *roba* (robe, dress, stuff): 'a showy wanton' (*OED*)
106–7 *in fresco* in the fresh air
109 *Canary* sweet wine from the Canary Islands
110 *spigot* wooden peg of a cask
111 *butt* cask
116 *French* ed. (Frenoh Q1)

WILLMORE

Damn the hungry balderdash! Cheerful sack has a generous virtue in't inspiring a successful confidence, gives
eloquence to the tongue and vigour to the soul, and has,
in a few hours, completed all my hopes and wishes!   120
There's nothing left to raise a new desire in me. Come,
let's be gay and wanton – and gentlemen, study; study
what you want, for here are friends that will supply,
gentlemen [*he jingles coins*]. Hark, what a charming
sound they make! 'Tis he and she gold whil'st here, and   125
shall beget new pleasures every moment.

BLUNT

But hark'ee, sir, you are not married are you?

WILLMORE

All the honey of matrimony, but none of the sting,
friend. – doesn't seek marridge rather sex –

BLUNT

'Sheartlikins, thou'rt a fortunate rogue!   130

WILLMORE

I am so, sir; let these [*chinking the coins*] inform you! Ha,
how sweetly they chime! Pox of poverty: it makes a man
a slave, makes wit and honour sneak. My soul grew lean
and rusty for want of credit.

BLUNT

'Sheartlikins, this I like well; it looks like my lucky   135
bargain! Oh, how I long for the approach of my squire
that is to conduct me to her house again. Why, here's
two provided for!

FREDERICK

By this light, y'are happy men.

BLUNT

Fortune is pleased to smile on us, gentlemen – to smile   140
on us.

> *Enter* SANCHO *and pulls down* BLUNT *by the*
> *sleeve. They go aside*

SANCHO

Sir, my lady expects you. She has removed all that might
oppose your will and pleasure – and is impatient till you
come.

---

117 *hungry balderdash* deficient jumbled mixture of liquors
     sack white wine from Spain and the Canaries
118 *confidence, gives* confidence which gives
125 *he and she* C2 (he and the Q1, Q2, C; the he and the she Q3)
     whil'st i.e. whilest, passes time idly

BLUNT

    Sir, I'll attend you. – Oh, the happiest rogue! I'll take   145
no leave, lest they either dog me or stay me.

Exit with SANCHO

BELVILE

    But then the little gipsy is forgot?

WILLMORE

    A mischief on thee for putting her into my thoughts. I
had quite forgot her else, and this night's debauch had
drunk her quite down.   150

HELLENA

    Had it so, good captain!

Claps him on the back

WILLMORE (*Aside*)

    Ha! I hope she did not hear me. – *guilty.*

HELLENA

    What, afraid of such a champion?

WILLMORE

    Oh, you're a fine lady of your word, are you not? To
make a man languish a whole day –   155

HELLENA

    In tedious search of me.

WILLMORE

    Egad, child, thou'rt in the right. Hadst thou seen what   *trying to*
a melancholy dog I have been ever since I was a lover,   *please her*
how I have walked the streets like a Capuchin, with my
hands in my sleeves – faith, sweetheart, thou wouldst   160
pity me.

HELLENA (*Aside*)

    Now, if I should be hanged I can't be angry with him,   *realises his*
he dissembles so heartily. – Alas, good captain, what   *infidelity*
pains you have taken; now were I ungrateful not to
reward so true a servant.   165

WILLMORE

    Poor soul, that's kindly said! I see thou bearest a con-
science. Come then, for a beginning, show me thy dear
face.

HELLENA

    I'm afraid, my small acquaintance, you have been staying

---

146 *dog* follow
159 *Capuchin* a hooded friar of the order of St Francis's austere new rule, 1528
166 *bearest* C (barest Q1–3)
169 *small acquaintance* i.e. person I have known only slightly
    staying sustaining, strengthening

that swinging stomach you boasted of this morning. I   170
then remember my little collation would have gone down
with you without the sauce of a handsome face. Is your
stomach so queasy now?

WILLMORE

Faith, long fasting, child, spoils a man's appetite. Yet, if
you durst treat, I could so lay about me still –   175

HELLENA

And would you fall to before a priest says grace?

WILLMORE

Oh, fie, fie, what an old, out of-fashioned thing hast
thou named? Thou couldst not dash me more out of
countenance shouldst thou show me an ugly face.

Whilst he is seemingly courting HELLENA, *enter* ANGELLICA,
MORETTA, BISKEY, *and* SEBASTIAN, *all in masquerade.*
ANGELLICA *sees* WILLMORE *and stares*

ANGELLICA

Heavens, 'tis he! And passionately fond to see another   180
woman!

MORETTA

What could you less expect from such a swaggerer?

ANGELLICA

Expect? As much as I paid him – a heart entire
Which I had pride enough to think, when'er I gave,
It would have raised the man above the vulgar,   185
Made him all soul, and that all soft and constant!

HELLENA

You see, captain, how willing I am to be friends with
you, till time and ill luck make us lovers, and ask you
the question first, rather than put your modesty to the
blush by asking me. For, alas! I know you captains are   190
such strict men, and such severe observers of your vows
to chastity, that 'twill be hard to prevail with your tender
conscience to marry a young willing maid!

WILLMORE

Do not abuse me, for fear I should take thee at thy word
and marry thee indeed, which I'm sure will be revenge   195
sufficient.

171 *collation* light meal that needs little preparation
173 *queasy* 1) easily upset 2) uncertain
176 *fall to* i.e. begin eating
179 s.d. 3 *stares* Q1–3 (starts C)
180 *'tis* Q3 ('ts Q1, it's Q2, is't C)

HELLENA

O' my conscience, that will be our destiny because we
are both of one humour. I am as inconstant as you, for
I have considered, captain, that a handsome woman has
a great deal to do whilst her face is good, for then is our 200
harvest-time to gather friends; and should I, in these
days of my youth, catch a fit of foolish constancy, I were
undone: 'tis loitering by daylight in our great journey.
Therefore I declare, I'll allow but one year for love, one
year for indifference, and one year for hate, and then – 205
go hang yourself – for I protest myself the gay, the kind,
and the inconstant. The devil's in't if this won't please
you.

WILLMORE

Oh, most damnably. I have a heart with a hole quite
through it, too; no prison, mine, to keep a mistress in. 210

ANGELLICA (*Aside*)

Perjured man! How I believe thee now. *– realising her mistake.*

HELLENA *– both made for each other – bold and quick witted.*

Well, I see our business as well as humours are alike:
yours to cozen as many maids as will trust you, and I as
many men as have faith. See if I have not as desperate a
lying look as you can have for the heart of you. (*Pulls* 215
off her vizard: he starts) How do you like it, captain?

WILLMORE

Like it! By Heaven, I never saw so much beauty! Oh,
the charms of those sprightly black eyes! That strangely
fair face, full of smiles and dimples! Those soft, round,
melting cherry lips and small, even, white teeth! Not to 220
be expressed, but silently adored! [*She replaces her mask*]
Oh, one look more, and strike me dumb or I shall repeat
nothing else till I'm mad!

He seems to court her to pull off her vizor: she refuses

ANGELLICA

I can endure no more. Nor is it fit to interrupt him, for
if I do, my jealousy has so destroyed my reason, I shall 225
undo him. Therefore I'll retire – and you, Sebastian (*to*
one of her bravos), follow that woman and learn who 'tis;
while you (*to the other bravo*) tell the fugitive I would
speak to him instantly.   *Exit*

This while FLORINDA [*in disguise*] *is talking to* BELVILE,
who stands sullenly, FREDERICK *courting* VALERIA

VALERIA

Prithee, dear stranger, be not so sullen, for though you 230

have lost your love, you see my friend frankly offers you
hers to play with in the meantime.

BELVILE
Faith, madam, I am sorry I can't play at her game.

FREDERICK
Pray leave your intercession and mind your own affair.
They'll better agree apart; he's a modest sigher in   235
company, but alone, no woman 'scapes him.

FLORINDA [*Aside*]
Sure, he does but rally – yet if it should be true? I'll
tempt him farther. – Believe me, noble stranger, I'm no
common mistress. And for a little proof on't – wear this
jewel. Nay, take it, sir, 'tis right, and bills of exchange   240
may sometimes miscarry.

BELVILE
Madam, why am I chosen out of all mankind to be the
object of your bounty?

VALERIA
There's another civil question asked.

FREDERICK
Pox of's modesty; it spoils his own markets and hinders   245
mine.

FLORINDA
Sir, from my window I have often seen you, and women
of my quality have so few opportunities for love that we
ought to lose none.

FREDERICK
Ay, this is something! Here's a woman! When shall I be   250
blessed with so much kindness from your fair mouth?
(*Aside to* BELVILE) – Take the jewel, fool.

BELVILE
You tempt me strangely, madam, every way.

FLORINDA (*Aside*)
So, if I find him false, my whole repose is gone.

BELVILE
And but for a vow I've made to a very fair lady, this   255
goodness had subdued me.

FREDERICK [*Aside to* BELVILE]
Pox on't, be kind; in pity to me, be kind, for I am to

---

237 *rally* banter, make fun (of Belvile)
240 *jewel* her portrait in miniature, in a locket or on a chain. She may be attempting
   to hang this round his neck.
   bills of exchange written orders to pay a given sum on a specified date
242 *chosen* ed. (chose Q1)
255 *fair* some copies Q1 (B.L.644.g.12), Q3 (om. some copies Q1, Q2, C)

thrive here but as you treat her friend.

HELLENA [*To* WILLMORE]

Tell me what you did in yonder house, and I'll unmask.

WILLMORE

Yonder house? Oh – I went to – a – to – why, there's a 260
friend of mine lives there.

HELLENA

What, a she or a he friend? ~ suspicious.

WILLMORE

A man upon honour! A man. – A she friend? No, no,
madam, you have done my business, I thank you.

HELLENA

And was't your man friend that had more darts in's eyes 265
than Cupid carries in's whole budget of arrows?

WILLMORE

So –

HELLENA

'Ah, such a *bona roba*! To be in her arms is lying in *fresco*,
all perfumed air about me.' – Was this your man friend
too?   270

WILLMORE

So –

HELLENA

That gave you the he and the she gold that begets young
pleasures?

WILLMORE

Well, well, madam, then you see there are ladies in the
world that will not be cruel. There are, madam, there 275
are – ~ trying to win over Hellena.

HELLENA

And there be men, too, as fine, wild, inconstant fellows
as yourself. There be, captain, there be, if you go to that
now. Therefore I'm resolved –

WILLMORE

Oh!   280

HELLENA

To see your face no more –   playing with Willmore
                               ↳ doesn't want him to
WILLMORE   disrespect her.

Oh!

HELLENA

Till tomorrow.

WILLMORE

Egad, you frighted me.

266 *budget* quiver
272 *the . . . gold* See l. 125.

HELLENA

Nor then neither, unless you'll swear never to see that   285
lady more. *- like AB requires assurance.*

WILLMORE

See her! Why, never to think of womankind again.

HELLENA

Kneel – and swear. *- forceful .*

[WILLMORE] *kneels; she gives him her hand*

WILLMORE

I do – never to think, to see, to love, nor lie – with any
but thyself.   290

HELLENA

Kiss the book.

WILLMORE

Oh, most religiously.

Kisses her hand

HELLENA

Now, what a wicked creature am I, to damn a proper
fellow.

CALLIS (*To* FLORINDA)

Madam, I'll stay no longer; 'tis e'en dark.   295

FLORINDA [*To* BELVILE]

However, sir, I'll leave this with you – that when I'm
gone, you may repent the opportunity you have lost by
your modesty.

Gives him the jewel, which is her picture, and exits.
He gazes after her

WILLMORE [*To* HELLENA]

'Twill be an age till tomorrow – and till then, I will most
impatiently expect you. Adieu, my dear, pretty angel.   300
Exeunt all the women

BELVILE

Ha! Florinda's picture! 'Twas she herself – what a dull
dog was I! I would have given the world for one minute's
discourse with her.

FREDERICK

This comes of your modesty! Ah, pox o' your vow; 'twas
ten to one but we had lost the jewel by't.   305

289 *I do – never . . . think, . . . see, . . . love,* ed. (I do never . . . think – to see – to love –
    nor Lye Q1)
291 *kiss . . . book* as if swearing on the Bible, here replaced by her hand

BELVILE

Willmore! The blessed'st opportunity lost! Florinda! Friends! Florinda!

WILLMORE

Ah, rogue! Such black eyes! Such a face! Such a mouth! Such teeth – and so much wit!

BELVILE

All, all, and a thousand charms besides.   310

WILLMORE

Why, dost thou know her?

BELVILE

Know her! Ay, ay, and a pox take me with all my heart for being modest.

WILLMORE

But hark'ee, friend of mine, are you my rival? And have I been only beating the bush all this while?   315

BELVILE

I understand thee not. I'm mad – see here –

Shows the picture [of FLORINDA]

WILLMORE

Ha! Whose picture's this? 'Tis a fine wench!   *still hasn't learned.*

FREDERICK

The colonel's mistress, sir.

WILLMORE

Oh, oh, here – (*gives the picture back*). I thought 't had been another prize. Come, come, a bottle will set thee   320 right again.

BELVILE

I am content to try, and by that time 'twill be late enough for our design.

WILLMORE

Agreed.

Love does all day the soul's great empire keep,   325
But wine at night lulls the soft god asleep.

Exeunt

315 *beating the bush* i.e. so that the game (Hellena) will be roused and driven towards Belvile rather than himself
325-6 Perhaps the final lines are sung off-stage.

[Act III,] Scene ii

Lucetta's house
Enter BLUNT *and* LUCETTA *with a light*

LUCETTA

Now we are safe and free; no fears of the coming home
of my old jealous husband, which made me a little
thoughtful when you came in first – but now love is all
the business of my soul.

BLUNT (*Aside*)

I am transported! Pox on't that I had but some fine   5
things to say to her, such as lovers use – I was a fool not to
learn of Fred a little by heart before I came. Something I
must say. [*To her*] – 'Sheartlikins, sweet soul! I am not
used to compliment, but I'm an honest gentleman, and
thy humble servant.   10

LUCETTA

I have nothing to pay for so great a favour, but such a *making use of*
love as cannot but be great, since at first sight of that *him by flattery*
sweet face and shape it made me your absolute captive.

naive and   BLUNT [*Aside*]
unwary of   Kind heart! How prettily she talks! Egad, I'll show her
her possible husband a Spanish trick; send him out of the world and   15
nature.   marry her: she's damnably in love with me, and will
                ne'er mind settlements, and so there's that saved.

LUCETTA

Well, sir, I'll go and undress me, and be with you
instantly.

BLUNT

Make haste then, for 'adsheartlikins, dear soul, thou   20
canst not guess at the pain of a longing lover when his
joys are drawn within the compass of a few minutes.

LUCETTA

You speak my sense, and I'll make haste to prove it.

Exit

BLUNT

'Tis a rare girl, and this one night's enjoyment with her
will be worth all the days I ever passed in Essex! Would   25
she would go with me into England; though, to say truth,
there's plenty of whores already. But a pox on 'em, they

15 *Spanish* i.e. synonymous with 'treacherous' to the English at this time
17 *settlements* the settling of property upon a person, e.g. before marriage
20 *'adsheartlikins* By God's little heart (see I.ii.14 note)
22 *drawn* drawn out
23 *prove* Q1, Q3 (provide Q2 and C, where the speech is an aside)

are such mercenary, prodigal whores, that they want
such a one as this, that's free and generous, to give 'em
good examples. – Why, what a house she has; how rich   30
and fine!

Enter SANCHO

SANCHO
Sir, my lady has sent me to conduct you to her chamber.
BLUNT
Sir, I shall be proud to follow. – Here's one of her
servants, too! 'Sheartlikins, by this garb and gravity he
might be a Justice of Peace in Essex, and is but a pimp   35
here.

Exeunt [BLUNT *and* SANCHO]

[Act III, Scene iii]

The scene changes to a chamber with an alcove bed in't, a table, etc.,
LUCETTA *in bed. Enter* SANCHO *and* BLUNT, *who takes the candle*
of SANCHO *at the door*

SANCHO
Sir, my commission reaches no farther.   [*Exit*]
BLUNT
Sir, I'll excuse your compliment. [*He locks the door after*
SANCHO] – What, in bed, my sweet mistress?
LUCETTA
You see, I still out-do you in kindness.
BLUNT
And thou shalt see what haste I'll make to quit scores –   5
oh, the luckiest rogue!

He undresses himself

LUCETTA
Should you be false or cruel now!
BLUNT
False! 'Sheartlikins, what dost thou take me for? A Jew?
An insensible heathen? A pox of thy old jealous husband;
an he were dead – egad, sweet soul – it should be none   10
of my fault if I did not marry thee. – desperation.
LUCETTA
It never should be mine.
BLUNT
Good soul! I'm the fortunatest dog!

35 *Justice of Peace* an important official in the seventeenth century

LUCETTA
  Are you not undressed yet?
BLUNT
  As much as my impatience will permit.   15

        Goes towards the bed in his shirt [and] drawers

LUCETTA
  Hold, sir, put out the light; it may betray us else.
BLUNT
  Anything! I need no other light but that of thine eyes! –
  'Sheartlikins, there, I think I had it.

        [He] puts out the candle; the bed descends;
                he gropes about to find it

  Why, why – where am I got? What, not yet? – Where are
  you, sweetest? – Ah, the rogue's silent now. A pretty   20
  love-trick, this – how she'll laugh at me anon! You need
  not, my dear rogue! You need not! I'm all on fire
  already. – Come, come, now call me in pity. – Sure, I'm
  enchanted! I have been round the chamber and can find
  neither woman, nor bed. I locked the door; I'm sure she   25
  cannot go that way – or if she could, the bed could not. –
  Enough, enough, my pretty wanton; do not carry the
  jest too far. (*Lights on a trap and is let down*) – Ha,
  betrayed! Dogs! Rogues! Pimps! – Help! Help!

        Enter LUCETTA, PHILIPPO, *and* SANCHO *with a light*

PHILIPPO
  Ha, ha, ha! He's dispatched finely.   30
LUCETTA
  Now, sir, had I been coy, we had missed of this booty.
PHILIPPO
  Nay, when I saw 'twas a substantial fool, I was mollified;
  but when you dote upon a serenading coxcomb, upon a
  face, fine clothes, and a lute, it makes me rage.
LUCETTA
  You know I was never guilty of that folly, my dear   35
  Philippo, but with yourself – but come, let's see what we
  have got by this.

---

18 s.d. 1 *bed descends* i.e. beneath the stage, through a trapdoor operated by machin-
   ery under the stage. See Introduction: The Play in Performance.
28 s.d. *Lights ... down* Blunt stands on a trapdoor which, when activated, drops
   him into the space below the stage (perhaps the concealed bed breaks his fall if
   the same trap is used).
30 *dispatched* ed. (dispatch Q1)

PHILIPPO

A rich coat – sword and hat! – These breeches, too, are
well- lined. – See here, a gold watch! – A purse, ha! Gold!
At least two hundred pistoles! – A bunch of diamond　　40
rings, and one with the family arms! – A gold box, with
a medal of his king, and his lady mother's picture! These
were sacred relics, believe me! – See, the waistband of
his breeches have a mine of gold – old Queen Bess's! We
have a quarrel to her ever since eighty-eight, and may,　　45
therefore, justify the theft: the Inquisition might have
committed it.

LUCETTA

– See, a bracelet of bowed gold! These, his sisters tied
about his arm at parting. But well – for all this, I fear his
being a stranger may make a noise and hinder our trade　　50
with them hereafter.

PHILIPPO

That's our security; he is not only a stranger to us, but
to the country, too. The common sewer into which he
is descended, thou knowest, conducts him into another
street, which this light will hinder him from ever finding　　55
again. He knows neither your name, nor that of the
street where your house is; nay, nor the way to his own
lodgings.

LUCETTA

And art not thou an unmerciful rogue? Not to afford
him one night for all this! I should not have been such a　　60
Jew.

PHILIPPO

Blame me not, Lucetta, to keep as much of thee as I can
to myself. Come, that thought makes me wanton! Let's
to bed! – Sancho, lock up these.

　　This is the fleece which fools do bear,　　　　　　65
　　Designed for witty men to shear.
　　　　　　　　　　Exeunt [LUCETTA, PHILIPPO, *and* SANCHO]

---

42 *his king* Charles II
45 *eighty-eight* 1588, the year of the Spanish Armada's defeat
48 *bowed* curved
53 *sewer* ed. (shoar Q1)

[Act III, Scene iv]

The scene changes, and discovers BLUNT *creeping*
out of a common sewer, his face, etc. all dirty

BLUNT *climbing up*

Oh Lord! I am got out at last and, which is a miracle,
without a clue. And now to damning and cursing! But
if that would ease me, where shall I begin? With my
fortune, myself, or the quean that cozened me? What a
dog was I to believe in Woman? Oh, coxcomb! Ignorant,   5
conceited coxcomb! To fancy she could be enamoured
with my person! At first sight, enamoured! Oh, I'm
a cursed puppy! 'Tis plain, 'Fool' was writ upon my
forehead! She perceived it – saw the Essex calf there.
For what allurements could there be in this countenance,   10
which I can endure because I'm acquainted with it? Oh,
dull, silly dog! To be thus soothed into a cozening! Had
I been drunk, I might fondly have credited the young
quean! But as I was in my right wits, to be thus cheated
confirms it I am a dull, believing, English country fop. –   15
But my comrades! Death and the devil, there's the worst
of all! Then a ballad will be sung tomorrow on the
Prado, to a lousy tune of the Enchanted Squire and the
Annihilated Damsel. – But Fred, that rogue, and the
colonel will abuse me beyond all Christian patience!   20
Had she left me my clothes, I have a bill of exchange at
home would've saved my credit – but now all hope is
taken from me. Well, I'll home – if I can find the
way – with this consolation, that I am not the first kind,
believing coxcomb, but there are, gallants, many such   25
good natures amongst ye.

And though you've better arts to hide your follies,
'Adsheartlikins, y'are all as arrant cullies.   [*Exit*]

---

0 s.d. 1 *discovers* reveals
  s.d. 2 *sewer* ed. (shoar Q1)
4 *quean* hussy (queen C)
  cozened See II.i.71 note.
5 *Woman* Q1–3 (Women C)
  coxcomb See I.i.123 note.
9 *Essex calf* See II.i.86–7 note.
15 *confirms it I* Q1, Q3 (confirms I Q2, C)
18 *Prado* a fashionable promenade, i.e. a popular public place
28 *cullies* dupes, simpletons
  s.d. Q3 (om. Q1, Q2, C)

[Act III,] Scene [v]

The garden in the night
Enter FLORINDA in an undress, with a key
and a little box

FLORINDA
Well, thus far I'm in my way to happiness. I have got
myself free from Callis; my brother, too, I find by yonder
light, is got into his cabinet and thinks not of me. I have,
by good fortune, got the key of the garden back-door.
I'll open it to prevent Belvile's knocking: a little noise   5
will now alarm my brother. Now am I as fearful as a
young thief. (*Unlocks the door*) – Hark! What noise is
that? Oh, 'twas the wind that played amongst the boughs.
Belvile stays long, methinks – it's time. Stay, for fear of
a surprise, I'll hide these jewels in yonder jasmine.   10

She goes to lay down the box

Enter WILLMORE drunk

WILLMORE
What the devil is become of these fellows, Belvile and
Frederick? They promised to stay at the next corner
for me, but who the devil knows the corner of a full
moon? Now, whereabouts am I? – Ha, what have we
here? A garden! A very convenient place to sleep in. – Ha,   15
what has God sent us here? A female – by this light, a
woman! I'm a dog if it be not a very wench!
FLORINDA
He's come! – Ha, who's there?
WILLMORE
Sweet soul, let me salute thy shoe-string!
FLORINDA [*Aside*]
'Tis not my Belvile. Good Heavens! I know him not. –   20
Who are you, and from whence come you?
WILLMORE
Prithee, prithee, child – not so many hard questions. Let
it suffice I am here, child. – Come, come kiss me.
FLORINDA
Good gods! What luck is mine?

---

0 s.d. 2 *an undress* partial or incomplete clothing

3 *cabinet* a small private apartment

12 *stay* See I.i.211 note.

WILLMORE

Only good luck, child, parlous good luck. Come hither. –   25
'Tis a delicate, shining wench! By this hand, she's perfumed, and smells like any nosegay. – Prithee, dear soul,
let's not play the fool and lose time, precious time; for
as Gad shall save me, I'm as honest a fellow as breathes,
though I'm a little disguised at present. – Come, I say. –   30
Why, thou may'st be free with me; I'll be very secret. I'll
not boast who 'twas obliged me, not I – for hang me if I
know thy name.

FLORINDA

Heavens! What a filthy beast is this?

WILLMORE

I am so, and thou ought'st the sooner to lie with me for   35
that reason. For look you, child, there will be no sin in't
because 'twas neither designed, nor premeditated. 'Tis
pure accident on both sides – that's a certain thing now.
Indeed, should I make love to you, and you vow fidelity –
and swear and lie till you believed and yielded – that   40
were to make it wilful fornication, the crying sin of
the nation. Thou art, therefore – as thou art a good
Christian – obliged in conscience to deny me nothing.
Now – come, be kind without any more idle prating.

FLORINDA

Oh, I am ruined! – Wicked man, unhand me.   45

WILLMORE

Wicked! Egad, child, a judge, were he young and vigorous, and saw those eyes of thine, would know 'twas
they gave the first blow – the first provocation. Come,
prithee, let's lose no time, I say. This is a fine, convenient
place.   50

FLORINDA

Sir, let me go, I conjure you, or I'll call out.

WILLMORE

Ay, ay, you were best to call witness to see how finely
you treat me. Do.

FLORINDA

I'll cry murder, rape, or anything if you do not instantly
let me go!   55

WILLMORE

A rape! Come, come, you lie, you baggage, you lie.
What, I'll warrant you would fain have the world believe

25 *parlous* extraordinary
30 *disguised* drunk
40–2 *that ... nation* Q1–3 (om. C)

now that you are not so forward as I. No, not you! –
Why, at this time of night, was your cobweb door set
open, dear spider, but to catch flies? Ha, come – or I　　60
shall be damnably angry. Why, what a coil is here.

FLORINDA

Sir, can you think –

WILLMORE

That you would do't for nothing? Oh, oh, I find what
you would be at. – Look here, here's a pistole for you.
Here's a work indeed. – Here, take it, I say.　　65

FLORINDA

For Heaven's sake, sir, as you're a gentleman –

WILLMORE

So – now, now, she would be wheedling me for more!
What, you will not take it then? You are resolved you
will not? Come, come take it or I'll put it up again – for
look ye, I never give more. Why, how now mistress, are　　70
you so high i'th' mouth a pistole won't down with you?
Ha, why, what a work's here! – In good time. Come, no
struggling to be gone. – But an y'are good at a dumb
wrestle I'm for ye. Look ye, I'm for ye –

She struggles with him

Enter BELVILE *and* FREDERICK

BELVILE

The door is open; a pox of this mad fellow. I'm angry　　75
that we've lost him; I durst have sworn he had followed
us.

FREDERICK

But you were so hasty, colonel, to be gone.

FLORINDA

Help! Help! Murder! Help – oh, I am ruined!

BELVILE

Ha! Sure, that's Florinda's voice. (*Comes up to them*) –　　80
A man! Villain, let go that lady.

A noise. WILLMORE *turns and draws;*
FREDERICK *interposes*

FLORINDA

Belvile! Heavens! My brother, too, is coming, and 'twill

61 *coil* turmoil, confusion
64 *pistole* See II.ii.41.
69 *up* away
71 *high i'th' mouth* See II.ii.30 note.
　　down 1) go down, i.e. satisfy 2) cause you to go down, i.e. lie with me
73 *an* if

be impossible to escape. – Belvile, I conjure you to walk
under my chamber window, from whence I'll give you
some instructions what to do. This rude man has undone   85
us!   *Exit*

WILLMORE
  Belvile!

  Enter PEDRO, STEPHANO, *and other servants, with lights*

PEDRO
  I'm betrayed! Run, Stephano, and see if Florinda be
  safe.

                                                    Exit STEPHANO

        They fight and Pedro's party beats 'em out.
                    [*Enter* STEPHANO]

  So, whoe'er they be, all is not well. (*Going out* [*he*] *meets*   90
  STEPHANO) I'll to Florinda's chamber.
STEPHANO
  You need not, sir, the poor lady's fast asleep and thinks
  no harm. I would not awake her, sir, for fear of frighting
  her with your danger.
PEDRO
  I'm glad she's there. – Rascals, how came the garden   95
  door open?
STEPHANO
  That question comes too late, sir – some of my fellow
  servants masquerading, I'll warrant.
PEDRO
  Masquerading! A lewd custom to debauch our youth.
  There's something more in this than I imagine.   100
                          Exeunt [PEDRO and STEPHANO]

[Act III, Scene vi]

            Scene changes to the street
      Enter BELVILE *in rage,* FREDERICK *holding him,*
                and WILLMORE, *melancholy*

WILLMORE
  Why, how the devil should I know Florinda?
BELVILE
  Ah, plague of your ignorance! If it had not been Florinda,
  must you be a beast – a brute, a senseless swine?

[handwritten annotations: "– still does not realise repercussion"; "→ Belvile contrasts to Willmore in his condemnation of his actions."]

93 *awake* Q1, Q2, C (wake Q3)

WILLMORE

Well, sir, you see I am endued with patience – I can
bear. Though, egad, y'are very free with me, methinks.   5
I was in good hopes the quarrel would have been on my
side, for so uncivilly interrupting me.

BELVILE

Peace, brute! Whilst thou'rt safe – oh, I'm distracted.

WILLMORE

Nay, nay, I'm an unlucky dog, that's certain.

BELVILE

Ah, curse upon the star that ruled my birth – or what-   10
soever other influence that makes me still so wretched!

[feels he has lost Florinda forever.]

WILLMORE

Thou break'st my heart with these complaints. There is
no star in fault, no influence but sack, the cursed sack I
drunk.

FREDERICK

Why, how the devil came you so drunk?   15

WILLMORE

Why, how the devil came you so sober?

BELVILE

A curse upon his thin skull; he was always beforehand
that way.

FREDERICK

[far more understanding]
Prithee, dear colonel, forgive him; he's sorry for his fault.

BELVILE

He's always so after he has done a mischief – a plague   20
on all such brutes! *[– is not the first time Willmore has done such a thing.]*

WILLMORE

By this light, I took her for an arrant harlot. *[→ believes it would have been fine that way.]*

BELVILE

Damn your debauched opinion! Tell me, sot, hadst thou
so much sense and light about thee to distinguish her
woman, and couldst not see something about her face   25
and person to strike an awful reverence into thy soul?

WILLMORE

Faith, no; I considered her as mere a woman as I could
wish.

BELVILE

'Sdeath, I have no patience – draw, or I'll kill you.

---

14 *drunk* Q1, Q3 (drank Q2, C)
17 *beforehand* ready in advance, anticipating – i.e. the opportunity to seduce a
   woman
22 *arrant* See II.i.82 note.
26 *awful* respectful

WILLMORE
> Let that alone till tomorrow, and if I set not all right   30
> again, use your pleasure.

BELVILE
> Tomorrow! Damn it,
> The spiteful light will lead me to no happiness.
> Tomorrow is Antonio's, and perhaps
> Guides him to my undoing. Oh, that I could meet   35
> This rival, this powerful fortunate!

WILLMORE
> What then?

BELVILE
> Let thy own reason, or my rage instruct thee.

WILLMORE
> I shall be finely informed then, no doubt. Hear me,
> colonel, hear me. Show me the man and I'll do his   40
> business.

BELVILE
> I know him no more than thou, or if I did, I should not
> need thy aid.

WILLMORE
> This, you say, is Angellica's house. I promised the kind
> baggage to lie with her tonight.   *Offers to go in*   45

> *Enter* ANTONIO *and his page.* ANTONIO *knocks*
> *on the hilt of's sword*

ANTONIO
> You paid the thousand crowns I directed?

PAGE
> To the lady's old woman, sir, I did.

WILLMORE
> Who the devil have we here?

BELVILE
> I'll now plant myself under Florinda's window, and if I
> find no comfort there, I'll die.   50
> *Exeunt* BELVILE *and* FREDERICK

> *Enter* MORETTA

MORETTA
> Page!

PAGE
> Here's my lord.

45 s.d. 2 *knocks* ed. (knock Q1)

WILLMORE

How is this? A picaroon going to board my frigate?
Here's one chase gun for you.

Drawing his sword, [he] jostles ANTONIO, *who turns
and draws. They fight.* ANTONIO *falls*

MORETTA

Oh, bless us! We're all undone!   55

Runs in and shuts the door

PAGE

Help! Murder!

Enter BELVILE *at the noise of fighting*

BELVILE

Ha! The mad rogue's engaged in some unlucky adventure again. — common behaviour

Enter two or three masqueraders

MASQUERADER

Ha! A man killed!

WILLMORE

How? A man killed! Then I'll go home to sleep.   60

*Puts up [his sword] and reels out.
Exeunt masqueraders another way*

BELVILE

Who should it be? Pray Heaven the rogue is safe, for all
my quarrel to him.

As BELVILE *is groping about, enter an* OFFICER
and six SOLDIERS

SOLDIER

Who's there?

OFFICER

So, here's one dispatched. Secure the murderer.

BELVILE

Do not mistake my charity for murder! I came to his   65
assistance.

SOLDIERS *seize on* BELVILE

OFFICER

That shall be tried, sir. – St Jago! Swords drawn in the
carnival time!

53 *picaroon* See II.ii.168 note.   54 *chase gun* naval gun used in pursuit
56 s.d. *Enter* BELVILE ed. (Belvile returns Q1)
67 *St Jago* St Iago (St James)

Goes to ANTONIO

ANTONIO
Thy hand, prithee.
OFFICER
Ha! Don Antonio! Look well to the villain, there. – How   70
is it, sir?
ANTONIO
I'm hurt.
BELVILE
Has my humanity made me a criminal?
OFFICER
Away with him.
BELVILE
What a cursed chance is this?   75
Exeunt SOLDIERS *with* BELVILE
ANTONIO (*To the* OFFICER)
This is the man that has set upon me twice. Carry him
to my apartment till you have further orders from me.
Exeunt [OFFICER *and*] ANTONIO, *led*

Act IV, Scene i

A fine room [*with a table*]
Discovers BELVILE *as by dark alone*

BELVILE
When shall I be weary of railing on fortune, who is
resolved never to turn with smiles upon me? Two such
defeats in one night none but the devil and that mad
rogue could have contrived to have plagued me with. I   5
am here a prisoner – but where, Heaven knows. And if
there be murder done, I can soon decide the fate of a
stranger in a nation without mercy. Yet this is nothing
to the torture my soul bows with when I think of losing
my fair, my dear Florinda. Hark, my door opens. – A
light! A man – and seems of quality. Armed, too! Now   10
shall I die like a dog without defence.

Enter ANTONIO *in a nightgown, with a light; his arm in a
scarf, and a sword under his arm: he sets the candle on the
table*

0 s.d. 2 *as . . . alone* as if in the dark

ANTONIO
    Sir, I come to know what injuries I have done you, that
    could provoke you to so mean an action as to attack me
    basely, without allowing time for my defence?
BELVILE
    Sir, for a man in my circumstances to plead innocence,   15
    would look like fear – but view me well and you will find
    no marks of coward on me; not anything that betrays
    that brutality you accuse me with.
ANTONIO
    In vain, sir, you impose upon my sense. You are not only
    he who drew on me last night, but yesterday before the   20
    same house, that of Angellica. Yet there is something in
    your face and mien that makes me wish I were mistaken.
BELVILE
    I own I fought today in the defence of a friend of mine
    with whom you, if you're the same, and your party, were
    first engaged. Perhaps you think this crime enough to   25
    kill me, but if you do, I cannot fear you'll do it basely.
ANTONIO
    No, sir, I'll make you fit for a defence with this.

                    Gives him the sword

BELVILE
    This gallantry surprises me – nor know I how to use this
    present, sir, against a man so brave.
ANTONIO
    You shall not need; for know, I come to snatch you from   30
    a danger that is decreed against you: perhaps your life,
    or long imprisonment. And 'twas with so much courage
    you offended, I cannot see you punished.
BELVILE
    How shall I pay this generosity?
ANTONIO
    It had been safer to have killed another than have   35
    attempted me. To show your danger, sir, I'll let you
    know my quality: and 'tis the viceroy's son whom you
    have wounded.

19–22 prose ed. (verse Q1)
25–6 *Perhaps ... me,* separate line in Q1
26 *but ... basely.* prose ed. (verse Q1)
    fear i.e. 'fear but'
30–72 prose ed. (verse Q1)
37 *quality* social rank

BELVILE

    The viceroy's son! (*Aside*) Death and confusion! Was
    this plague reserved to complete all the rest? Obliged by   40
    him – the man of all the world I would destroy!

ANTONIO

    You seem disordered, sir.

BELVILE

    Yes, trust me, sir, I am, and 'tis with pain that man
    receives such bounties, who wants the power to pay 'em
    back again.   45

ANTONIO

    To gallant spirits 'tis indeed uneasy; but you may quickly
    overpay me, sir.

BELVILE (*Aside*)

    Then I am well, kind Heaven! But set us even, that I
    may fight with him and keep my honour safe. [*To*
    ANTONIO] – Oh, I'm impatient, sir, to be discounting the   50
    mighty debt I owe you. Command me quickly.

ANTONIO

    I have a quarrel with a rival, sir, about the maid we love.

BELVILE (*Aside*)

    Death, 'tis Florinda he means – that thought destroys
    my reason, and I shall kill him!

ANTONIO

    My rival, sir, is one has all the virtues man can boast   55
    of –

BELVILE (*Aside*)

    Death! Who should this be?

ANTONIO

    He challenged me to meet him on the Molo as soon as
    day appeared, but last night's quarrel has made my arm
    unfit to guide a sword.   60

BELVILE

    I apprehend you, sir. You'd have me kill the man that
    lays a claim to the maid you speak of. I'll do't. I'll fly to
    do't!

ANTONIO

    Sir, do you know her?

BELVILE

    No, sir, but 'tis enough she is admired by you.   65

ANTONIO

    Sir, I shall rob you of the glory on't, for you must fight

44 *wants* See I.ii.10 note.
50 *discounting* repaying
58 s.p. ANTONIO Q3, C2 (om. Q1)

under my name and dress.

BELVILE

That opinion must be strangely obliging that makes you
think I can personate the brave Antonio, whom I can
but strive to imitate.   70

ANTONIO

You say too much to my advantage. Come, sir, the day
appears that calls you forth. Within, sir, is the habit.
                                                        Exit

BELVILE

Fantastic fortune, thou deceitful light,
That cheats the wearied traveller by night,
Though on a precipice each step you tread,   75
I am resolved to follow where you lead.   *Exit*

[Act IV,] Scene [ii]

The Molo
Enter FLORINDA *and* CALLIS *in masks,*
with STEPHANO

FLORINDA (*Aside*)

I'm dying with my fears: Belvile's not coming as I
expected under my window, makes me believe that all
those fears are true. [*To* STEPHANO] – Canst thou not tell
with whom my brother fights?

STEPHANO

No, madam, they were both in masquerade. I was by   5
when they challenged one another, and they had decided
the quarrel then, but were prevented by some cavaliers;
which made 'em put it off till now – but I am sure 'tis
about you they fight.

FLORINDA (*Aside*)

Nay, then 'tis with Belvile, for what other lover have I   10
that dares fight for me, except Antonio, and he is too
much in favour with my brother. If it be he, for whom
shall I direct my prayers to Heaven?

STEPHANO

Madam, I must leave you, for if my master see me, I
shall be hanged for being your conductor. I escaped   15
narrowly for the excuse I made for you last night i'th'
garden.

72 *habit* clothes, i.e. to disguise him
1–4 prose ed. (Makes ... true. / – Canst ... fights? Q1)
15 *I* C2 (om. Q1–3, C)

FLORINDA
And I'll reward thee for't. Prithee, no more.

Exit STEPHANO

Enter DON PEDRO *in his masking habit*

PEDRO
Antonio's late today; the place will fill, and we may be
prevented.   20

Walks about

FLORINDA (*Aside*)
Antonio? Sure, I heard amiss. – unexpected.
PEDRO
But who will not excuse a happy lover
When soft, fair arms confine the yielding neck,
And the kind whisper languishingly breathes,
'Must you be gone so soon?'   25
Sure I had dwelt forever on her bosom –
But stay, he's here.

Enter BELVILE *dressed in Antonio's clothes*

FLORINDA (*Aside*)
'Tis not Belvile; half my fears are vanished.
PEDRO
Antonio!
BELVILE (*Aside*)
This must be he. [*To* PEDRO] – You're early, sir; I do not   30
use to be outdone this way.
PEDRO
The wretched, sir, are watchful, and 'tis enough you've
the advantage of me in Angellica.
BELVILE (*Aside*)
Angellica! Or I've mistook my man, or else Antonio!
Can he forget his interest in Florinda and fight for   35
common prize? – surprised due to previous thought
                              that he was in love with Florinda
PEDRO
Come, sir, you know our terms.
BELVILE (*Aside*)
By Heaven, not I! [*To* PEDRO] – No talking; I am ready,
sir.

[BELVILE] *offers to fight;* FLORINDA *runs in*

30–1 lineation ed. (This . . . he. / – You're . . . way. Q1)
32–3 prose ed. (verse Q1)
34 *Or . . . or* Either . . . or

FLORINDA (*To* BELVILE)

    Oh, hold! Whoe'er you be, I do conjure you hold! If you   40
    strike here, I die.

PEDRO

    Florinda!

BELVILE

    Florinda imploring for my rival!

PEDRO

    Away; this kindness is unseasonable.

> *Puts her by; they fight; she runs in just as*
> BELVILE *disarms* PEDRO

FLORINDA

    Who are you, sir, that dares deny my prayers?   45

BELVILE

    Thy prayers destroy him. If thou wouldst preserve him,
    Do that thou'rt unacquainted with, and curse him.

> *She holds* BELVILE

FLORINDA

    By all you hold most dear, by her you love,
    I do conjure you: touch him not.

BELVILE

    By her I love!
    See – I obey – and at your feet resign   50
    The useless trophy of my victory.

> *Lays his sword at her feet*

PEDRO

    Antonio, you've done enough to prove you love Florinda.

BELVILE

    Love Florinda! Does Heaven love adoration, prayer, or
    penitence? Love her! Here, sir, your sword again.   55

> *Snatches up the sword and gives it to him*

    Upon this truth I'll fight my life away.

PEDRO

    No, you've redeemed my sister, and my friendship.

> *He gives him* FLORINDA *and pulls off his vizard to*
> *show his face, and puts it on again*

BELVILE

    Don Pedro!

45 *dares* (dare Q2, C)

PEDRO
　Can you resign your claims to other women,
　And give your heart entirely to Florinda?　　　　　60
BELVILE
　Entire, as dying saints' confessions are!
　I can delay my happiness no longer.
　This minute, let me make Florinda mine!
PEDRO
　This minute let it be – no time so proper!
　This night my father will arrive from Rome,　　　65
　And possibly may hinder what we purpose.
FLORINDA
　Oh, Heavens! This minute!

　　　　Enter masqueraders and pass over [*the stage*]

BELVILE [*Aside*]
　Oh, do not ruin me!
PEDRO
　The place begins to fill, and that we may not be observed,
　do you walk off to St Peter's Church, where I will meet　70
　you, and conclude your happiness.
BELVILE
　I'll meet you there. (*Aside*) – If there be no more saints'
　churches in Naples.
FLORINDA
　Oh, stay, sir, and recall your hasty doom!
　Alas, I have not prepared my heart　　　　　75
　To entertain so strange a guest.
PEDRO
　Away; this silly modesty is assumed too late.
BELVILE
　Heaven, madam, what do you do?
FLORINDA
　Do? Despise the man that lays a tyrant's claim
　To what he ought to conquer by submission.　　　80
BELVILE
　You do not know me – move a little this way.

　　　　　Draws her aside

FLORINDA
　Yes, you may force me even to the altar,
　But not the holy man that offers there
　Shall force me to be thine.

　　　　PEDRO *talks to* CALLIS *this while*

BELVILE
　Oh, do not lose so blest an opportunity.　　　　85

See – 'tis your Belvile – not Antonio
Whom your mistaken scorn and anger ruins!

Pulls off his vizard

FLORINDA
Belvile!
Where was my soul it could not meet thy voice
And take this knowledge in?   90

As they are talking, enter WILLMORE, *finely dressed,
and* FREDERICK

WILLMORE
No intelligence? No news of Belvile yet? Well, I am the
most unlucky rascal in nature. Ha! Am I deceived, or is
it he? Look Fred, 'tis he – my dear Belvile.

*Runs and embraces him. Belvile's vizard
falls out on's hand*

BELVILE
Hell and confusion seize thee!
PEDRO
Ha! Belvile! I beg your pardon, sir.   95

Takes FLORINDA *from him*

BELVILE
Nay, touch her not. She's mine by conquest, sir;
I won her by my sword.
WILLMORE
Didst thou so? And, egad, child, we'll keep her by the
sword.

Draws on PEDRO. BELVILE *goes between* [*them*]

BELVILE
Stand off!   100
Thou'rt so profanely lewd, so cursed by Heaven,
All quarrels thou espousest must be fatal.
WILLMORE
Nay, an you be so hot, my valour's coy,
And shall be courted when you want it next.

Puts up his sword

---

91 *intelligence* tidings
93 *Fred,* ed. (Ferd – Q1; as s.p. Q2, C, C2, with following sentence assigned)
103–4 verse ed. (prose Q1)
103 *an* See III.v.73 note.

BELVILE (*To* PEDRO)
    You know I ought to claim a victor's right.   105
    But you're the brother to divine Florinda,
    To whom I'm such a slave: to purchase her
    I durst not hurt the man she holds so dear.

PEDRO
    'Twas by Antonio's, not by Belvile's sword
    This question should have been decided, sir.   110
    I must confess, much to your bravery's due,
    Both now, and when I met you last in arms.
    But I am nicely punctual in my word,
    As men of honour ought, and beg your pardon.
    For this mistake, another time shall clear.   115

        Aside to FLORINDA *as they are going out*

    This was some plot between you and Belvile.
    But I'll prevent you.

                    [*Exit with* FLORINDA]

        BELVILE *looks after her and begins to walk*
              up and down in rage

WILLMORE
    Do not be modest now and lose the woman; but if we
    shall fetch her back so –

BELVILE
    Do not speak to me!   120

WILLMORE
    Not speak to you! Egad, I'll speak to you, and will be
    answered too!

BELVILE
    Will you, sir!

WILLMORE
    I know I've done some mischief, but I'm so dull a puppy
    that I'm the son of a whore if I know how, or where.   125
    Prithee, inform my understanding.

BELVILE
    Leave me, I say, and leave me instantly.

WILLMORE
    I will not leave you in this humour, nor till I know my
    crime.

BELVILE
    Death, I'll tell you, sir –   130

112 *when . . . arms* i.e. at the siege
113 *nicely punctual* scrupulously definite
115 *clear* elucidate
123 *sir!* ed. (Sir – Q1)

Draws and runs at WILLMORE, *[who] runs out,*
BELVILE *after him;* FREDERICK *interposes [but does not follow*
them]
Enter ANGELLICA, MORETTA, *and* SEBASTIAN

ANGELLICA

Ha! – Sebastian, is that not Willmore? Haste, haste, and
bring him back.

[*Exit* SEBASTIAN]

→ rarely impossi [handwritten]

FREDERICK

The colonel's mad: I never saw him thus before. I'll after
'em, lest he do some mischief, for I am sure Willmore
will not draw on him.   *Exit* 135

ANGELLICA

I am all rage! My first desires defeated!
For one, for aught he knows, that has no   *realising that she* [handwritten]
Other merit than her quality –   *is caring for the* [handwritten]
Her being Don Pedro's sister. He loves her! *money cause* [handwritten]
I know 'tis so. Dull, dull, insensible –   140
He will not see me now, though oft invited,
And broke his word last night – false, perjured man!
He that but yesterday fought for my favours,
And would have made his life a sacrifice   *her cynical nature* [handwritten]
To've gained one night with me,   *about love* 145 [handwritten]
Must now be hired and courted to my arms. *returns.* [handwritten]

MORETTA

I told you what would come on't, but Moretta's an old,
doting fool. Why did you give him five hundred crowns,
but to set himself out for other lovers? You should have
kept him poor if you had meant to have had any good 150
from him.

ANGELLICA

Oh, name not such mean trifles. Had I given
Him all my youth has earned from sin,
I had not lost a thought, nor sigh upon't.
But I have given him my eternal rest,   155
My whole repose, my future joys, my heart!
My virgin heart, Moretta! Oh, 'tis gone!
suffers a broken heart [handwritten]

136 *all* Q1, Q2, C (om. Q3)
138 *quality* See IV.i.37 note.
140 *insensible* unintelligible
149 *set himself out* dress himself up
152–3 *Oh, ... Him all* (one line Q1–3, C, C2)

MORETTA
> Curse on him, here he comes; how fine she has made
> him, too.

Enter WILLMORE *and* SEBASTIAN. ANGELLICA
turns and walks away

WILLMORE
> How now, turned shadow! 160
> Fly when I pursue, and follow when I fly!

Sings

> Stay, gentle shadow of my dove
> And tell me ere I go,
> Whether the substance may not prove
> A fleeting thing like you. 165

As she turns, she looks on him

> There's a soft, kind look remaining yet.

ANGELLICA
> Well, sir, you may be gay: all happiness, all joys pursue
> you still. Fortune's your slave and gives you, every hour,
> choice of new hearts and beauties, till you are cloyed
> with the repeated bliss which others vainly languish for. 170
> But know, false man, that I shall be revenged.

Turns away in rage

WILLMORE
> So, gad, there are of those faint-hearted lovers, whom
> such a sharp lesson next their hearts would make as
> impotent as fourscore. Pox o' this whining – my business
> is to laugh and love – a pox on't! I hate your sullen lover: 175
> a man shall lose as much time to put you in humour
> now, as would serve to gain a new woman.

ANGELLICA
> I scorn to cool that fire I cannot raise,
> Or do the drudgery of your virtuous mistress.

WILLMORE
> A virtuous mistress! Death, what a thing thou hast found 180
> out for me! Why, what the devil should I do with a
> virtuous woman – a sort of ill-natured creatures, that
> take a pride to torment a lover? Virtue is but an infirmity
> in woman, a disease that renders even the handsome
> ungrateful; whilst the ill-favoured, for want of sol- 185
> icitations and address, only fancy themselves so. I have

158–9 prose ed. (Curse . . . comes; / How . . . too. Q1)

lain with a woman of quality, who has all the while been
railing at whores.

ANGELLICA
I will not answer for your mistress's virtue,
Though she be young enough to know no guilt;   190
And I could wish you would persuade my heart
'Twas the two hundred thousand crowns you courted.

WILLMORE
Two hundred thousand crowns! What story's this? What
trick? What woman? – Ha!

ANGELLICA
How strange you make it; have you forgot the creature   195
you entertained on the Piazzo last night?

WILLMORE (*Aside*)
Ha! My gipsy worth two hundred thousand crowns! Oh,
how I long to be with her. Pox, I knew she was of quality.

ANGELLICA
False man! I see my ruin in thy face.
How many vows you breathed upon my bosom,   200
Never to be unjust. Have you forgot so soon?

WILLMORE
Faith no; I was just coming to repeat 'em. (*Aside*) – But
here's a humour indeed would make a man a saint.
Would she would be angry enough to leave me, and
command me not to wait on her.   205

Enter HELLENA *dressed in man's clothes*

HELLENA [*Aside*]
This must be Angellica! I know it by her mumping
matron here – ay, ay, 'tis she! My mad captain's with
her, too, for all his swearing. How this unconstant
humour makes me love him! [*To* MORETTA] – Pray, good,
grave gentlewoman, is not this Angellica?   210

MORETTA
My too-young-sir, it is. [*Aside*] – I hope 'tis one from
Don Antonio.

Goes to ANGELLICA

HELLENA (*Aside*)
Well, something I'll do to vex him for this.

ANGELLICA
I will not speak with him; am I in humour to receive a
lover?   215

195 *How ... make it* How you affect indignation about it
206 *mumping* grimacing, miserable
208 *unconstant* Q1, Q3 (inconstant Q2, C, C2); i.e. unfaithful in love

WILLMORE

Not speak with him! Why, I'll be gone, and wait your
idler minutes. Can I show less obedience to the thing I
love so fondly?

Offers to go

ANGELLICA

A fine excuse this! Stay!

WILLMORE

And hinder your advantage! Should I repay your boun-   220
ties so ungratefully?

ANGELLICA [*To* HELLENA]

Come hither, boy [*to* WILLMORE] – that I may let you see
How much above the advantages you name
I prize one minute's joy with you.

WILLMORE (*impatient to be gone*)

Oh, you destroy me with this endearment.   225
(*Aside*) – Death! How shall I get away? – Madam, 'twill
not be fit I should be seen with you. – Besides, it will
not be convenient – and I've a friend – that's dangerously
sick.

ANGELLICA

I see you're impatient – yet you shall stay.   230

WILLMORE (*Aside*)

And miss my assignation with my gipsy.

Walks about impatiently. MORETTA *brings*
HELLENA, *who addresses herself to* ANGELLICA

HELLENA

Madam,
You'll hardly pardon my intrusion
When you shall know my business!
And I'm too young to tell my tale with art;   235
But there must be a wondrous store of goodness
Where so much beauty dwells.

ANGELLICA

A pretty advocate whoever sent thee.
Prithee proceed. (*To* WILLMORE *who is stealing off*)
                              – Nay, sir, you shall not go.

WILLMORE (*Aside*)

Then I shall lose my dear gipsy forever.   240
Pox on't; she stays me out of spite.

[HELLENA]

I am related to a lady, madam,

231 s.d. *Walks* ... ANGELLICA ed. (*Aside, and walks* ... *Angellica* Q1)
242 s.p. HELLENA ed. (Ang. Q1)

Young, rich, and nobly born, but has the fate
To be in love with a young English gentleman.
Strangely she loves him: at first sight she loved him,   245
But did adore him when she heard him speak; *manipulating him*
For he, she said, had charms in every word, *by praising him and*
That failed not to surprise, to wound and conquer. *his words.*

WILLMORE (*Aside*)

Ha! Egad, I hope this concerns me.

ANGELLICA

'Tis my false man he means: would he were gone.   250
This praise will raise his pride, and ruin me. (*To*
    WILLMORE) — Well,
Since you are so impatient to be gone,
I will release you, sir.

WILLMORE (*Aside*)

Nay, then I'm sure 'twas me he spoke of; this cannot be
the effects of kindness in her.   255
— No, madam, I've considered better on't,
And will not give you cause of jealousy. — *does not want a scene*

ANGELLICA

But, sir, I've — business that —

WILLMORE

This shall not do; I know 'tis but to try me.

ANGELLICA

Well, to your story, boy (*aside*) — though 'twill undo me.   260

HELLENA

With this addition to his other beauties,
He won her unresisting, tender heart. *describing the way*
He vowed, and sighed, and swore he loved her dearly; *he won all the*
And she believed the cunning flatterer, *other women*
And thought herself the happiest maid alive.   265
Today was the appointed time by both
To consummate their bliss;
The virgin, altar, and the priest were dressed,
And while she languished for th'expected bridegroom,
She heard he paid his broken vows to you.   270

WILLMORE [*Aside*]

So, this is some dear rogue that's in love with me, and
this way lets me know it; or if it be not me, he means
someone whose place I may supply. — *seeking a way out*
↳ flirts continued

ANGELLICA

Now I perceive
The cause of thy impatience to be gone,   275

---

271 s.d. *Aside* C2 (om. Q1–3, C)
271–2 prose ed. (verse Q1)

And all the business of this glorious dress.

WILLMORE
Damn the young prater; I know not what he means.

HELLENA
Madam,
In your fair eyes I read too much concern
To tell my farther business.   280

ANGELLICA
Prithee, sweet youth, talk on; thou may'st perhaps
Raise here a storm that may undo my passion,
And then I'll grant thee anything.

HELLENA
Madam, 'tis to entreat you (oh, unreasonable!)
You would not see this stranger;   285
For if you do, she vows you are undone,
Though nature never made a man so excellent,
And sure, he 'ad been a god, but for inconstancy.

WILLMORE (*Aside*)
Ah, rogue, how finely he's instructed!
'Tis plain; some woman that has seen me *en passant*.   290

ANGELLICA
Oh, I shall burst with jealousy! Do you know the man
you speak of?

HELLENA
Yes, madam; he used to be in buff and scarlet.

ANGELLICA (*To* WILLMORE)
Thou, false as Hell, what canst thou say to this?

WILLMORE
By Heaven –   295

ANGELLICA
Hold, do not damn thyself –

HELLENA
Nor hope to be believed.

          He walks about; they follow

ANGELLICA
Oh, perjured man!
Is't thus you pay my generous passion back?

HELLENA
Why would you, sir, abuse my lady's faith?   300

ANGELLICA
And use me so inhumanely.

277 *prater* idle chatterer
290 *en passant* in passing
301 *inhumanely* Q2, Q3, C, C2 (unhumanely Q1)

HELLENA
  A maid so young, so innocent –
WILLMORE
  Ah, young devil.
ANGELLICA
  Dost thou not know thy life is in my power?
HELLENA
  Or think my lady cannot be revenged?   305
WILLMORE (*Aside*)
  So, so, the storm comes finely on.
ANGELLICA
  Now thou art silent; guilt has struck thee dumb.
  Oh, hadst thou still been so, I'd lived in safety.

                  She turns away and weeps

WILLMORE (*Aside to* HELLENA)
  Sweet heart, the lady's name and house – quickly!
  I'm impatient to be with her.   310

            Looks towards ANGELLICA *to watch her turning,*
            and as she comes towards them, he meets her

HELLENA (*Aside*)
  So, now is he for another woman.
WILLMORE
  The impudent'st young thing in nature,
  I cannot persuade him out of his error, madam.
ANGELLICA
  I know he's in the right – yet thou'st a tongue
  That would persuade him to deny his faith.   315

                  In rage walks away

WILLMORE (*said softly to* HELLENA)
  Her name, her name, dear boy –
HELLENA
  Have you forgot it, sir?
WILLMORE (*Aside*)
  Oh, I perceive he's not to know I am a stranger to his
  lady.
  – Yes, yes, I do know, but I have forgot the – (ANGELLICA   320
    turns).
  – By Heaven, such early confidence I never saw.

303 *devil* ed. (Divel Q1)
304 *in my* Q2, Q3, C, C2 (my Q1)
308 *still* always (*OED* 7b)
312 *impudent'st* ed. (impudents Q1)

ANGELLICA

Did I not charge you with this mistress, sir?
Which you denied, though I beheld your perjury.
This little generosity of thine has rendered back my
     heart.

Walks away

WILLMORE [*To* HELLENA]

So, you have made sweet work here, my little mischief;   325
look your lady be kind and good natured now, or I shall
have but a cursed bargain on't.

(ANGELLICA *turns towards them*)

– The rogue's bred up to mischief;
Art thou so great a fool to credit him?

ANGELLICA

Yes, I do, and you in vain impose upon me.   330
[*To* HELLENA] – Come hither, boy. Is not this he you
     spake of?

HELLENA

I think – it is; I cannot swear, but I vow he has just such
another lying lover's look.

HELLENA *looks in his face; he gazes on her*

WILLMORE

Ha! Do not I know that face?
(*Aside*) – By Heaven, my little gipsy! What a dull dog   335
was I. Had I but looked that way, I'd known her. Are all
my hopes of a new woman banished? [*To* HELLENA] –
Egad, if I do not fit thee for this, hang me. [*To* ANG-
ELLICA] – Madam, I have found out the plot.

HELLENA [*Aside*]

Oh lord, what does he say? Am I discovered now?   340

WILLMORE

Do you see this young spark here?

HELLENA [*Aside*]

He'll tell her who I am.

WILLMORE

Who do you think this is?

HELLENA [*Aside*]

Ay, ay, he does know me. [*To* WILLMORE] – Nay, dear
captain! I am undone if you discover me.   345

325–9 verse in Q1
331 *spake* Q1 (speak Q2, Q3, C, C2)

WILLMORE

Nay, nay, no cogging. She shall know what a precious
mistress I have.

HELLENA

Will you be such a devil?

WILLMORE

Nay, nay, I'll teach you to spoil sport you will not make.
[*To* ANGELLICA] – This small ambassador comes not from   350
a person of quality as you imagine, and he says – but
from a very arrant gipsy, the talking'st, prating'st, canting'st little animal thou ever saw'st.

ANGELLICA

What news you tell me; that's the thing I mean.

HELLENA (*Aside*)

Would I were well off the place; if ever I go a-captain-   355
hunting again –

WILLMORE

Mean that thing? That gipsy thing? Thou may'st as well
be jealous of thy monkey or parrot as of her. A German
motion were worth a dozen of her, and a dream were a
better enjoyment – a creature of a constitution fitter for   360
Heaven than man. ~ *finally managing to outwit Helena.*

HELLENA (*Aside*)

Though I'm sure he lies, yet this vexes me.

ANGELLICA

You are mistaken; she's a Spanish woman
Made up of no such dull materials.

WILLMORE

Materials! Egad, an she be made of any that will either   365
dispense or admit of love, I'll be bound to continence.

HELLENA (*Aside to him*)

Unreasonable man, do you think so?

[WILLMORE] (*To* HELLENA)

You may return, my little brazen head, and tell your lady
that till she be handsome enough to be beloved, or I dull
enough to be religious, there will be small hopes of me.   370

ANGELLICA

Did you not promise, then, to marry her?   *gets her out of the way → has control and submits to her.*

WILLMORE

Not I, by Heaven.

346 *cogging* wheedling
352 *arrant* See II.i.82 note.
359 *motion* puppet (i.e. automaton)
366 *continence* restraint in relation to sexual appetite
368 s.p. WILLMORE Q3, C, C2 (om. Q1, Q2)

ANGELLICA
You cannot undeceive my fears and torments till you
have vowed you will not marry her.

HELLENA (*Aside*)
If he swears that, he'll be revenged on me indeed for all   375
my rogueries. — will not forgive him for denying
her.

ANGELLICA
I know what arguments you'll bring against me – fortune,
and honour.

WILLMORE
Honour! I tell you, I hate it in your sex; and those that
fancy themselves possessed of that foppery are the most   380
impertinently troublesome of all womankind, and will
transgress nine commandments to keep one, and to
satisfy your jealousy, I swear –

HELLENA (*Aside to him*)
Oh, no swearing, dear captain.

WILLMORE
describing   If it were possible I should ever be inclined to marry, it   385
Hellena   should be some kind young sinner; one that has gen-
rather than   erosity enough to give a favour handsomely to one that
AB.   can ask it discreetly; one that has wit enough to manage
an intrigue or love. Oh, how civil such a wench is to a
man that does her the honour to marry her.   390

ANGELLICA
By Heaven there's no faith in anything he says.

Enter SEBASTIAN

SEBASTIAN
Madam, Don Antonio –

ANGELLICA
Come hither.

HELLENA [*Aside*]
Ha! Antonio! He may be coming hither and he'll
certainly discover me; I'll therefore retire without a   395
ceremony.   *Exit*

ANGELLICA
I'll see him; get my coach ready.

SEBASTIAN
It waits you, madam.

WILLMORE [*Aside*]
This is lucky. – What, madam, now I may be gone and
leave you to the enjoyment of my rival?   400

375 *swears that,* ed. (Swears, that Q1)

ANGELLICA

Dull man, that canst not see how ill, how poor,   *fully rejected*
That false dissimulation looks. Begone   *and without hope*
And never let me see thy cozening face again,
Lest I relapse and kill thee.

WILLMORE

Yes, you can spare me now. Farewell, till you're in better   405
humour. [*Aside*] – I'm glad of this release.
Now for my gipsy:
For though to worse we change, yet still we find
New joys, new charms, in a new miss that's kind.   *Exit*

ANGELLICA

He's gone, and in this ague of my soul   410
The shivering fit returns.
Oh, with what willing haste he took his leave,
As if the longed-for minute were arrived
Of some blest assignation.
In vain I have consulted all my charms,   415
In vain this beauty prized, in vain believed
My eyes could kindle any lasting fires;
I had forgot my name, my infamy,
And the reproach that honour lays on those
That dare pretend a sober passion here.   420
Nice reputation, though it leave behind
More virtues than inhabit where that dwells;   *has taken away*
Yet that once gone, those virtues shine no more.   *her life by making*
Then since I am not fit to be beloved,   *her fall for this*
I am resolved to think on a revenge   425
On him that soothed me thus to my undoing.

Exeunt [SEBASTIAN *and* ANGELLICA]

[Act IV,] Scene iii

A street
Enter FLORINDA *and* VALERIA *in habits different*
from what they have been seen in

FLORINDA

We're happily escaped, and yet I tremble still.

VALERIA

A lover and fear! Why, I am but half an one, and yet I
have courage for any attempt. Would Hellena were here;

403 *cozening* deceitful
421 *nice* 1) strict, scrupulous 2) delicate
426 *soothed* flattered, cajoled

I would fain have had her as deep in this mischief as we.
She'll fare but ill else, I doubt.   5

FLORINDA

She pretended a visit to the Augustine nuns, but I believe
some other design carried her out; pray Heaven we light
on her. Prithee what didst do with Callis?

VALERIA

When I saw no reason would do good on her, I followed
her into the wardrobe, and as she was looking for some-   10
thing in a great chest, I toppled her in by the heels,
snatched the key of the apartment where you were confined, locked her in, and left her bawling for help.

FLORINDA

'Tis well you resolve to follow my fortunes, for thou
darest never appear at home again after such an action.   15

VALERIA

That's according as the young stranger and I shall agree.
But to our business. I delivered your letter, your note to
Belvile, when I got out under pretence of going to mass.
I found him at his lodging, and believe me it came
seasonably, for never was man in so desperate a con-   20
dition. I told him of your resolution of making your
escape today, if your brother would be absent long
enough to permit you; if not, to die rather than be
Antonio's.

FLORINDA

Thou should'st have told him I was confined to my   25
chamber upon my brother's suspicion that the business
on the Molo was a plot laid between him and I.

VALERIA

I said all this, and told him your brother was now gone
to his devotion, and he resolves to visit every church till
he find him, and not only undeceive him in that, but   30
caress him so as shall delay his return home.

FLORINDA

Oh, Heavens! He's here, and Belvile with him too.

They put on their vizards
Enter DON PEDRO, BELVILE, WILLMORE; BELVILE
and DON PEDRO *seeming in serious discourse*

6 *Augustine nuns* a Roman Catholic order, following the rule of St Augustine
8 *didst* i.e. didst thou
10 *wardrobe* dressing-room where clothing and costly objects were kept
17 *your letter, your note* Q1–3, C, C2; but some copies of Q1 give 'your note'.
27 *Molo* See II.i.217 note.
32 s.d. 1 *vizards* See II.i.0 s.d. 2 note.

VALERIA
Walk boldly by them, and I'll come at distance, lest he
suspect us.

She walks by them and looks back on them

WILLMORE
Ha! A woman, and of an excellent mien.   35
PEDRO
She throws a kind look back on you.
WILLMORE
Death! 'Tis a likely wench, and that kind look shall not
be cast away. I'll follow her.
BELVILE
Prithee do not.
WILLMORE
Do not? By Heavens, to the antipodes, with such an   40
invitation.

[VALERIA] *goes out and* WILLMORE *follows her*

BELVILE
'Tis a mad fellow for a wench.

Enter FREDERICK

FREDERICK
Oh, colonel, such news!
BELVILE
Prithee what?
FREDERICK
News that will make you laugh in spite of fortune.   45
BELVILE
What, Blunt has had some damned trick put upon him –
cheated, banged, or clapped?
FREDERICK
Cheated sir, rarely cheated of all but his shirt and
drawers; the unconscionable whore, too, turned him out
before consummation, so that, traversing the streets at   50
midnight, the watch found him in this *fresco*, and con-
ducted him home. By Heaven, 'tis such a sight, and yet
I durst as well been hanged as laughed at him, or pity
him; he beats all that do but ask him a question, and is
in such an humour.   55

35 *mien* 1) bearing 2) appearance
40 *Do not?* (Do not, Q1)
   antipodes the opposite side of the earth
47 *banged, or clapped* violently beaten, or infected with gonorrhea
48 *rarely* uncommonly, exceptionally
51 *fresco* See III.i.106–7 note.

PEDRO
  Who is't has met with this ill usage, sir?
BELVILE
  A friend of ours whom you must see for mirth's sake.
  (*Aside*) – I'll employ him to give Florinda time for an
  escape.
PEDRO
  What is he?   60
BELVILE
  A young countryman of ours, one that has been educated
  at so plentiful a rate, he yet ne'er knew the want of
  money; and 'twill be a great jest to see how simply he'll
  look without it. For my part, I'll lend him none; and the
  rogue know not how to put on a borrowing face and ask   65
  first, I'll let him see how good 'tis to play our parts whilst
  I play his. – Prithee, Fred, do you go home and keep
  him in that posture till we come.
                Exeunt [BELVILE, DON PEDRO, *and* FREDERICK]

          Enter FLORINDA *from the farther end of the scene,
                      looking behind her*

FLORINDA
  I am followed still. Ha! My brother, too, advancing this
  way. Good Heavens defend me from being seen by him.   70
                                                  She goes off

          Enter WILLMORE, *and after him,* VALERIA,
                      at a little distance

WILLMORE
  Ah! There she sails! She looks back as she were willing
  to be boarded; I'll warrant her prize.
                              He goes out, VALERIA *following*

          Enter HELLENA, *just as he goes out, with a* PAGE

HELLENA
  Ha! Is not that my captain that has a woman in chase?
  'Tis not Angellica. [*To* PAGE] – Boy, follow those people
  at a distance, and bring me an account where they go   75
  in.
                                                  Exit PAGE
  [*Aside*] – I'll find his haunts and plague him everywhere.
  Ha! My brother!
                BELVILE, WILLMORE, [*and*] PEDRO *cross the stage;*
                                        HELLENA *runs off*

---

72 *warrant her prize* guarantee she's a ship I can legally capture (seize)

[Act IV, Scene iv]

Scene changes to another street
Enter FLORINDA

FLORINDA

What shall I do? My brother now pursues me. Will no
kind power protect me from his tyranny? – Ha, here's a
door open; I'll venture in, since nothing can be worse
than to fall into his hands. My life and honour are at
stake, and my necessity has no choice.   *Goes in*   5

[handwritten margin note: brother in power | I can make / break her.]

Enter VALERIA *and* HELLENA'S PAGE, *peeping after*
FLORINDA

PAGE

Here she went in; I shall remember this house.
                                                      Exit BOY

VALERIA

This is Belvile's lodging; she's gone in as readily as if she
knew it. Ha! Here's that mad fellow again; I dare not
venture in. I'll watch my opportunity.   *Goes aside*

Enter WILLMORE *gazing about him*

WILLMORE

I have lost her hereabouts. Pox on't, she must not 'scape   10
me so.   *Goes out*

[Act IV, Scene v]

Scene changes to Blunt's chamber, discovers him
sitting on a couch in his shirt and drawers, reading

BLUNT

So, now my mind's a little at peace, since I have resolved
revenge. A pox on this tailor, though, for not bringing
home the clothes I bespoke. And a pox of all poor
cavaliers; a man can never keep a spare suit for 'em, and
I shall have these rogues come in and find me naked,   5
and then I'm undone. But I'm resolved to arm myself –
the rascals shall not insult over me too much. (*Puts on
an old rusty sword and buff belt*) – Now, how like a morris
dancer I am equipped! A fine ladylike whore to cheat me
thus, without affording me a kindness for my money – a   10

0 s.d. 1 *discovers* See I.ii.227 note.
8–9 *morris dancer . . . equipped* i.e. how fantastically or grotesquely dressed I am

pox light on her. I shall never be reconciled to the sex
more; she has made me as faithless as a physician, as
uncharitable as a churchman, and as ill-natured as a
poet. Oh, how I'll use all womankind hereafter! What
would I give to have one of 'em within my reach now!   15
Any mortal thing in petticoats, kind fortune, send me,
and I'll forgive thy last night's malice. – Here's a cursed
book, too – 'A warning to all young travellers': that can
instruct me how to prevent such mischief now 'tis too
late! Well, 'tis a rare convenient thing to read a little now   20
and then, as well as hawk and hunt.

Sits down again and reads
Enter to him FLORINDA

FLORINDA
This house is haunted sure; 'tis well furnished and no
living thing inhabits it. Ha! – A man! Heavens, how he's
attired! Sure 'tis some rope-dancer or fencing master. I
tremble now for fear, and yet I must venture now to   25
speak to him. – Sir, if I may not interrupt your medi-
tations –

He starts up and gazes

BLUNT
Ha, what's here? Are my wishes granted? And is not that
a she creature? 'Adsheartlikins, 'tis! What wretched thing
art thou, ha?   30
FLORINDA
Charitable sir, you've told yourself already what I am; a
very wretched maid, forced by a strange unlucky accident to seek a safety here, and must be ruined if you do
not grant it.
BLUNT
Ruined! Is there any ruin so inevitable as that which now   35
threatens thee? Dost thou know, miserable woman, into
what den of mischiefs thou art fallen? What abyss of
confusion, ha? Dost not see something in my looks that
frights thy guilty soul, and makes thee wish to change
that shape of woman for any humble animal, or devil?   40
For those were safer for thee, and less mischievous.
FLORINDA
Alas, what mean you, sir? I must confess, your looks
have something in 'em makes me fear, but I beseech

18 *book* the one he was reading when the scene opened
27 s.d. *He* Q3, C, C2 (She Q1, Q2)   33–4 *and ... it* verse in Q1

you, as you seem a gentleman, pity a harmless virgin
that takes your house for sanctuary.   45

BLUNT
Talk on, talk on, and weep too, till my faith return. Do,
flatter me out of my senses again – a harmless virgin
with a pox; as much one as t'other, 'adsheartlikins. Why,
what the devil, can I not be safe in my house for you,
not in my chamber? Nay, even being naked, too, cannot   50
secure me: this is an impudence greater than has invaded
me yet. – Come, no resistance.

Pulls her rudely

FLORINDA
Dare you be so cruel?

BLUNT
Cruel, 'adsheartlikins, as a galley slave, or a Spanish
whore. Cruel? Yes, I will kiss and beat thee all over; kiss 55
and see thee all over; thou shalt lie with me too – not
that I care for the enjoyment, but to let thee see I have
ta'en deliberated malice to thee, and will be revenged
on one whore for the sins of another. I will smile and
deceive thee, flatter thee and beat thee, kiss and swear,   60
and lie to thee, embrace thee and rob thee, as she did
me, fawn on thee, and strip thee stark naked; then hang
thee out at my window by the heels, with a paper of
scurvy verses fastened to thy breast in praise of damnable
women. – Come, come along!   65

FLORINDA
Alas, sir, must I be sacrificed for the crimes of the most
infamous of my sex? I never understood the sins you
name.

BLUNT
Do, persuade the fool you love him, or that one of you
can be just or honest; tell me I was not an easy coxcomb,   70
or any strange, impossible tale: it will be believed sooner
than thy false showers or protestations. A generation of
damned hypocrites to flatter my very clothes from my
back! Dissembling witches! Are these the returns you
make an honest gentleman that trusts, believes, and   75
loves you? But if I be not even with you. – Come along –
or I shall –

Pulls her again

58 *ta'en* C2 ('tain' Q1, Q2, C; 'tame' some copies Q1; 'taken' Q3)
70 *coxcomb* See I.i.123 note.

Enter FREDERICK

FREDERICK
   Ha! What's here to do?
BLUNT
   'Adsheartlikins, Fred, I am glad thou art come, to be a
   witness of my dire revenge.   80
FREDERICK
   What's this, a person of quality too, who is upon the
   ramble to supply the defects of some grave impotent
   husband?
BLUNT
   No, this has another pretence; some very unfortunate
   accident brought her hither, to save a life pursued by I   85
   know not who, or why, and forced to take sanctuary
   here at Fool's Haven. 'Adsheartlikins, to me of all
   mankind for protection? Is the ass to be cajoled again,
   think ye? No, young one, no prayers or tears shall miti-
   gate my rage; therefore prepare for both my pleasures of   90
   enjoyment and revenge, for I am resolved to make up
   my loss here on thy body. I'll take it out in kindness and
   in beating.
FREDERICK
   Now, mistress of mine, what do you think of this?
FLORINDA
   I think he will not – dares not be so barbarous.   95
FREDERICK
   Have a care, Blunt, she fetched a deep sigh. She is
   enamoured with thy shirt and drawers; she'll strip thee
   even of that. There are, of her calling, such unconscionable baggages, and such dexterous thieves, they'll
   flay a man and he shall ne'er miss his skin till he feels   100
   the cold. There was a countryman of ours robbed of a
   row of teeth whilst he was a-sleeping, which the jilt made
   him buy again when he waked. – You see, lady, how little
   reason we have to trust you.
BLUNT
   'Dsheartlikins, why this is most abominable.   105
FLORINDA
   Some such devils there may be, but by all that's holy, I
   am none such; I entered here to save a life in danger.

90 *pleasures* Q1–3 (pleasure C, C2)
100 *flay* ed. (flea Q1)
102 *a-sleeping* Q1, Q2, C (sleeping Q3, C2)

BLUNT

For no goodness, I'll warrant her.

FREDERICK

Faith, damsel, you had e'en confessed the plain truth,
for we are fellows not to be caught twice in the same   110
trap. Look on that wreck, a tight vessel when he set out
of haven, well-trimmed and laden, and see how a female
picaroon of this island of rogues has shattered him, and
canst thou hope for any mercy?

BLUNT

No, no, gentlewoman, come along. 'Adsheartlikins, we   115
must be better acquainted. [*To* FREDERICK] – We'll both
lie with her, and then let me alone to bang her.

FREDERICK

I'm ready to serve you in matters of revenge that has a
double pleasure in't.

BLUNT

Well said. You hear, little one, how you are condemned   120
by public vote to the bed within; there's no resisting your
destiny, sweetheart.

Pulls her

FLORINDA

Stay, sir. I have seen you with Belvile, an English cavalier;
for his sake use me kindly. You know him, sir.

BLUNT

Belvile? Why yes, sweeting, we do know Belvile, and   125
wish he were with us now. He's a cormorant at whore
and bacon; he'd have a limb or two of thee, my virgin
pullet. But 'tis no matter; we'll leave him the bones to
pick.

FLORINDA

Sir, if you have any esteem for that Belvile, I conjure you 130
to treat me with more gentleness; he'll thank you for the
justice.

FREDERICK

Hark'ee, Blunt, I doubt we are mistaken in this matter.

FLORINDA

Sir, if you find me not worth Belvile's care, use me as

109 *confessed* Q1, Q2 (confess Q3, C, C2)
111 *tight* water-tight
113 *picaroon* See II.ii.168 note.
117 *bang* See I.ii.300 note.
118–19 *has . . . in't* i.e. have . . . in them
126–7 *cormorant . . . bacon* insatiably greedy devourer of whores and flesh

you please, and that you may think I merit better treat-   135
ment than you threaten, pray take this present –

Gives him a ring; he looks on it

BLUNT

Hum – a diamond! Why, 'tis a wonderful virtue now
that lies in this ring, a mollifying virtue. 'Adsheartlikins,
there's more persuasive rhetoric in't than all her sex can
utter.   140

FREDERICK

I begin to suspect something; and 'twould anger us vilely
to be trussed up for a rape upon a maid of quality, when
we only believe we ruffle a harlot.

BLUNT

Thou art a credulous fellow, but 'adsheartlikins I have
no faith yet. Why, my saint prattled as parlously as this   145
does; she gave me a bracelet, too – a devil on her – but
I sent my man to sell it today for necessaries, and it
proved as counterfeit as her vows of love.

FREDERICK

However, let it reprieve her till we see Belvile.

BLUNT

That's hard, yet I will grant it.   150

Enter a SERVANT

SERVANT

Oh, sir, the colonel is just come in with his new friend
and a Spaniard of quality, and talks of having you to
dinner with 'em.

BLUNT

'Dsheartlikins, I'm undone – I would not see 'em for
the world. Hark'ee, Fred, lock up the wench in your   155
chamber.

FREDERICK

Fear nothing, madam; whate'er he threatens, you are
safe whilst in my hands.

Exeunt FREDERICK *and* FLORINDA

BLUNT

And, sirrah, upon your life, say – I am not at home – or
that I am asleep – or – or anything. Away; I'll prevent   160
their coming this way.

Locks the door, and exeunt

143 *ruffle* handle with rude familiarity
145 *parlously* See I.ii.156 note.

Act V, Scene i

Blunt's chamber
After a great knocking at his chamber door, enter BLUNT
softly crossing the stage, in his shirt and drawers as before

[VOICES] (*call within*)
Ned, Ned Blunt, Ned Blunt!

BLUNT
The rogues are up in arms. 'Sheartlikins, this villainous
Frederick has betrayed me; they have heard of my
blessed fortune.

[VOICES] (*and knocking within*)
Ned Blunt! Ned, Ned –   5

BELVILE [*within*]
Why, he's dead, sir, without dispute, dead. He has not
been seen today. Let's break open the door. Here, boy –

BLUNT
Ha, break open the door. 'Dsheartlikins, that mad fellow
will be as good as his word.

BELVILE [*within*]
Boy, bring something to force the door.   10

A great noise within, at the door again

BLUNT
So, now must I speak in my own defence; I'll try what
rhetoric will do. [*To those without*] Hold, hold! What do
you mean, gentlemen? What do you mean?

BELVILE (*within*)
Oh, rogue, art alive? Prithee open the door and convince
us.   15

BLUNT
Yes, I am alive, gentlemen – but at present a little busy.

BELVILE (*within*)
How? Blunt grown a man of business? Come, come,
open and let's see this miracle.

BLUNT
No, no, no, no! Gentlemen, 'tis no great business – but –
I am – at – my devotion. 'Dsheartlikins, will you not   20
allow a man time to pray?

0 s.d. 1 *chamber* Q1–3 (room C, C2); see I.i.0 s.d. note.
1 s.p. VOICES ed. (not in Q1)
5 s.p. VOICES ed. (not in Q1)
   s.d. *and knocking* Q1, Q2, C, C2 (calling and knocking Q3)
19 *No, no, no, no* Q1, Q2, C, C2 (No, no, no Q3)

BELVILE (*within*) — doesn't believe him.

Turned religious! A greater wonder than the first, therefore open quickly, or we shall unhinge, we shall.

BLUNT [*Aside*]

This won't do. [*To them*] – Why, hark'ee colonel, to tell
you the plain truth, I am about a necessary affair of life –   25
I have a wench with me. You apprehend me? [*Aside*]
The devil's in't if they be so uncivil as to disturb me
now.

WILLMORE [*within*]

How, a wench? Nay, then we must enter and partake no
resistance – unless it be your lady of quality, and then   30
we'll keep our distance.

BLUNT [*Aside*]

So, the business is out.

WILLMORE [*within*]

Come, come, lend's more hands to the door. – Now
heave all together. (*Breaks open the door*) So, well done,
my boys!   35

    Enter BELVILE [*and his* PAGE], WILLMORE, FREDERICK,
    and PEDRO. BLUNT *looks simply; they all laugh at him. He*
    lays his hand on his sword and comes up to WILLMORE

BLUNT

Hark'ee, sir, laugh out your laugh quickly, d'ye hear,
and begone. I shall spoil your sport else. 'Adsheartlikins,
sir, I shall – the jest has been carried on too long. (*Aside*)
A plague upon my tailor!

WILLMORE

'Sdeath, how the whore has dressed him! Faith sir, I'm   40
sorry.

BLUNT

Are you so, sir? Keep't to yourself then, sir, I advise you,
d'ye hear, for I can as little endure your pity as his mirth.

    Lays his hand on's sword

BELVILE

Indeed, Willmore, thou wert a little too rough with Ned
Blunt's mistress. Call a person of quality, whore? And   45
one so young, so handsome, and so eloquent – ha, ha,
he.

33 *lend's* i.e. lend us Q1–3, C (lend C2)
35 s.d. 2 *simply* foolishly
36 *d'ye* (de ye Q1) The form has been changed throughout.
40 *Faith* i.e. in faith
46–7 *Ha, ha, he* Q1, Q2, C, C2 (Ha, ha, ha Q3)

BLUNT

Hark'ee, sir, you know me, and know I can be angry.
Have a care, for 'adsheartlikins, I can fight too – I can,
sir. Do you mark me? No more.   50

BELVILE

Why so peevish, good Ned? Some disappointments, I'll
warrant. What, did the jealous count, her husband,
return just in the nick? – *playing a dangerous game*

BLUNT

Or the devil, sir. (*They laugh*) – D'ye laugh? Look ye
settle me a good sober countenance, and that quickly   55
too, or you shall know Ned Blunt is not –

BELVILE

Not everybody; we know that.

BLUNT

Not an ass to be laughed at, sir.

WILLMORE

Unconscionable sinner, to bring a lover so near his
happiness – a vigorous passionate lover – and then not   60
only cheat him of his movables, but his very desires, too!

BELVILE

Ah! Sir, a mistress is a trifle with Blunt. He'll have a
dozen the next time he looks abroad. His eyes have
charms not to be resisted; there needs no more than to
expose that taking person to the view of the fair, and he   65
leads 'em all in triumph.

PEDRO

Sir, though I'm a stranger to you, I am ashamed at the
rudeness of my nation, and could you learn who did it,
would assist you to make an example of 'em.

BLUNT

Why, ay, there's one speaks sense now, and handsomely;   70
and let me tell you, gentlemen, I should not have showed
myself like a jack pudding, thus to have made you mirth,
but that I have revenge within my power. For know, I
have got into my possession a female who had better
have fallen under any curse than the ruin I design her.   75
'Adsheartlikins, she assaulted me here in my own lodgings, and had doubtless committed a rape upon me, had
not this sword defended me.

FREDERICK

I know not that, but o' my conscience thou had ravished

72 *jack pudding* buffoon, clown

her, had she not redeemed herself with a ring. Let's see   80
it, Blunt.

BLUNT shows the ring

BELVILE [*Aside*]
Ha! The ring I gave Florinda when we exchanged our
vows. – Hark'ee, Blunt –   *Goes to whisper to him*
WILLMORE
No whispering, good colonel. There's a woman in the
case, no whispering   85
BELVILE [*To* BLUNT]
Hark'ee, fool, be advised, and conceal both the ring and
the story for your reputation's sake. Do not let people
know what despised cullies we English are; to be cheated
and abused by one whore, and another rather bribe thee
than be kind to thee, is an infamy to our nation.   90
WILLMORE
Come, come, where's the wench? We'll see her; let her
be what she will, we'll see her.
PEDRO
Ay, ay, let us see her. I can soon discover whether she
be of quality, or for your diversion.
BLUNT
She's in Fred's custody.   95
WILLMORE [*To* FREDERICK]
Come, come, the key –

[FREDERICK] gives him the key; they are going

BELVILE [*Aside*]
Death, what shall I do? – Stay, gentlemen. [*Aside*] – Yet
if I hinder 'em I shall discover all. [*To them*] – Hold, let's
go one at once. Give me the key.
WILLMORE
Nay, hold there, colonel. I'll go first.   100
FREDERICK
Nay, no dispute; Ned and I have the propriety of her.
WILLMORE
Damn propriety – then we'll draw cuts. (BELVILE *goes*

80 *had* Q1, Q2 (hadst Q3, C, C2)
82 *exchanged* Q2, Q3, C, C2 (exchange Q1)
88 *cullies* See III.iv.28 note.
94 *quality* See I.ii.330 note.
98 *discover* See I.ii.227 note.
98–9 *let's go one* Q1, Q2, C, C2 (let one go Q3)
99 *one at once* one at a time
101 *propriety* Q2, Q3, C (property C2; gropriety Q1)

to whisper [to] WILLMORE) – Nay, no corruption, good
colonel. Come, the longest sword carries her.

They all draw, forgetting DON PEDRO, *being a Spaniard,
had the longest*

BLUNT

I yield up my int'rest to you, gentlemen, and that will   105
be revenge sufficient.

WILLMORE (*To* PEDRO)

The wench is yours. [*Aside*] – Pox of his Toledo, I had
forgot that.

FREDERICK

Come, sir, I'll conduct you to the lady.

Exeunt FREDERICK *and* PEDRO

BELVILE (*Aside*)

To hinder him will certainly discover her. [*To*] WILLMORE   110
[*who is*] *walking up and down out of humour* – Dost know,
dull beast, what mischief thou hast done?

WILLMORE

Ay, ay, to trust our fortune to lots! A devil on't; 'twas
madness, that's the truth on't.

BELVILE

Oh, intolerable sot –   115

Enter FLORINDA *running, masked,* PEDRO *after her:*
WILLMORE *gazing round her*

FLORINDA (*Aside*)

Good Heaven defend me from discovery.

PEDRO

'Tis but in vain to fly me; you're fallen to my lot.

BELVILE

Sure, she's undiscovered yet, but now I fear there is no
way to bring her off.

WILLMORE

Why, what a pox; is not this my woman? The same I   120
followed but now?

PEDRO *talking to* FLORINDA, *who walks up and down*

PEDRO

As if I did not know ye, and your business here.

FLORINDA (*Aside*)

Good Heaven, I fear he does indeed –

104 s.d. 1 *being* Q2, C, C2 (being as Q1, Q3)
106 *be* ed. (be; Q1)
107 *Toledo* a finely-tempered (and in this case, long) sword blade
110 s.d. *To* WILLMORE Q3 (Willmore Q1, Q2, C, C2)
119 *bring her off* procure her escape

PEDRO

Come, pray be kind. I know you meant to be so when
you entered here, for these are proper gentlemen.   125

WILLMORE

But sir – perhaps the lady will not be imposed upon.
She'll choose her man.

PEDRO

I am better bred than not to leave her choice free.

Enter VALERIA, *and is surprised at sight of* DON PEDRO

VALERIA (*Aside*)

Don Pedro here! There's no avoiding him.

FLORINDA (*Aside*)

Valeria! Then I'm undone –   130

VALERIA (*To* PEDRO, *running to him*)

Oh, have I found you, sir! The strangest accident – if I
had breath – to tell it.

PEDRO

Speak! Is Florinda safe? Hellena well?

VALERIA

Ay, ay, sir. Florinda – is safe [*aside*] – from any fears of
you.   135

PEDRO

Why, where's Florinda? Speak.

VALERIA

Ay, where indeed, sir. I wish I could inform you – but
to hold you no longer in doubt –

FLORINDA (*Aside*)

Oh, what will she say?

VALERIA

She's fled away in the habit – of one of her pages, sir –   140
but Callis thinks you may retrieve her yet, if you make
haste away. She'll tell you, sir, the rest (*aside*) – if you
can find her out.

PEDRO

Dishonourable girl! She has undone my aim. [*To
BELVILE*] – Sir, you see my necessity of leaving you, and   145
hope you'll pardon it. My sister, I know, will make her
flight to you; and if she do, I shall expect she should be
rendered back.

BELVILE

I shall consult my love and honour, sir.

                                               Exit PEDRO

125 *proper* See I.i.42 note.
146 *hope* Q1, Q3 (I hope Q2, C, C2)

FLORINDA (*To* VALERIA)
My dear preserver, let me embrace thee.   150
WILLMORE
What the devil's all this?
BLUNT
Mystery by this light.
VALERIA
Come, come, make haste and get yourselves married
quickly, for your brother will return again.
BELVILE
I'm so surprised with fears and joys, so amazed to find 155
you here in safety, I can scarce persuade my heart into
a faith of what I see.
WILLMORE
Hark'ee, colonel, is this that mistress who has cost you
so many sighs, and me so many quarrels with you?
BELVILE
It is. (*To* FLORINDA) Pray give him the honour of your 160
hand.
WILLMORE
Thus it must be received then.

Kneels and kisses her hand

And with it give your pardon too.
FLORINDA
The friend to Belvile may command me anything.
WILLMORE (*Aside*)
Death, would I might! 'Tis a surprising beauty.   165
BELVILE
Boy, run and fetch a Father instantly.

Exit BOY

FREDERICK
So, now do I stand like a dog, and have not a syllable to
plead my own cause with. By this hand, madam, I was
never thoroughly confounded before, nor shall I ever
more dare look up with confidence, till you are   170
pleased to pardon me.
FLORINDA
Sir, I'll be reconciled to you on one condition – that
you'll follow the example of your friend in marrying a
maid that does not hate you, and whose fortune (I
believe) will not be unwelcome to you.   175
FREDERICK
Madam, had I no inclinations that way, I should obey
your kind commands.

BELVILE

Who, Fred, marry? He has so few inclinations for
womankind, that had he been possessed of paradise, he
might have continued there to this day, if no crime but   180
love could have disinherited him.

FREDERICK

Oh, I do not use to boast of my intrigues.

BELVILE

Boast! Why, thou dost nothing but boast; and I dare
swear, wert thou as innocent from the sin of the grape
as thou art from the apple, thou might'st yet claim   185
that right in Eden which our first parents lost by too
much loving.

FREDERICK

I wish this lady would think me so modest a man.

VALERIA

She would be sorry then, and not like you half so well,
and I should be loath to break my word with you, which   190
was, that if your friend and mine agreed, it should be a
match between you and I.

She gives him her hand

FREDERICK

Bear witness, colonel, 'tis a bargain.   *Kisses her hand*

BLUNT (*To* FLORINDA)

I have a pardon to beg, too, but 'adsheartlikins, I am so
out of countenance that I'm a dog if I can say anything   195
to purpose.

FLORINDA

Sir, I heartily forgive you all.

BLUNT

That's nobly said, sweet lady. – Belvile, prithee present
her her ring again, for I find I have not courage to
approach her myself.   200

Gives him the ring; [BELVILE] *gives it to* FLORINDA
Enter BOY

BOY

Sir, I have brought the Father that you sent for.

BELVILE

'Tis well, and now my dear Florinda, let's fly to complete
that mighty joy we have so long wished and sighed for. –
Come Fred, you'll follow?

200 s.d. 1 *gives it to* Q3, C, C2 (ring he gives to Q1, Q2)

FREDERICK

Your example, sir, 'twas ever my ambition in war, and   205
must be so in love.

WILLMORE

And must not I see this juggling knot tied?

BELVILE

No, thou shalt do us better service and be our guard,
lest Don Pedro's sudden return interrupt the ceremony.

WILLMORE

Content – I'll secure this pass.   210

Exeunt BELVILE, FLORINDA, FREDERICK, *and* VALERIA

Enter BOY

BOY (*To* WILLMORE)

Sir, there's a lady without would speak to you.

WILLMORE

Conduct her in, I dare not quit my post.

BOY [*To* BLUNT]

And sir, your tailor waits you in your chamber.

BLUNT

Some comfort yet: I shall not dance naked at the
wedding.   215

Exeunt BLUNT *and* BOY

Enter again the BOY, *conducting in* ANGELLICA, *in a
masking habit and a vizard.* WILLMORE *runs to her*

WILLMORE

This can be none but my pretty gipsy. – Oh, I see you
can follow as well as fly. Come, confess thyself the most
malicious devil in nature; you think you have done my
business with Angellica –

ANGELLICA

Stand off, base villain –   220

She draws a pistol, and holds [it] to his breast

WILLMORE

Ha, 'tis not she! Who art thou, and what's thy business?

ANGELLICA

One thou hast injured, and who comes to kill thee for't.

WILLMORE

What the devil canst thou mean?

ANGELLICA

By all my hopes to kill thee –

*Holds still the pistol to his breast; he going back,
she following still*

207 *juggling* deceitful

WILLMORE
    Prithee, on. What acquaintance? For I know thee not.   225
ANGELLICA
    Behold this face – so lost to thy remembrance!

Pulls off her vizard

    And then call all thy sins about thy soul,
    And let 'em die with thee.
WILLMORE
    Angellica!
ANGELLICA
    Yes, traitor,   230
    Does not thy guilty blood run shivering through thy
        veins?
    Hast thou no horror at this sight that tells thee
    Thou hast not long to boast thy shameful conquest?
WILLMORE
    Faith, no, child; my blood keeps its old ebbs and flows
    still, and that usual heat too, that could oblige thee with 235
    a kindness, had I but opportunity.
ANGELLICA
    Devil! Dost wanton with my pain? – Have at thy heart!
WILLMORE
    Hold, dear virago! Hold thy hand a little;
    I am not now at leisure to be killed. Hold, and hear me.
    (*Aside*) – Death, I think she's in earnest.   240
ANGELLICA (*Aside, turning from him*)
    Oh, if I take not heed,
    My coward heart will leave me to his mercy.
    – What have you, sir, to say? – But should I hear thee,
    Thou'ldst talk away all that is brave about me:

Follows him with the pistol to his breast

    And I have vowed thy death by all that's sacred.   245
WILLMORE
    Why then, there's an end of a proper handsome fellow,
    That might 'a lived to have done good service yet.
    – That's all I can say to't.
ANGELLICA (*pausingly*)
    Yet – I would give thee – time for – penitence.

225 *Prithee, on. What* ed. ('Prithee on, what' Q1, Q2; 'Prithee on what' Q3, C, C2)
230 *traitor* Q2, Q3, C, C2 (tailor Q1)
238 *virago* heroic woman, female warrior
244 *Thou'ldst* ed. (Thoud'st Q1)
247 *'a* i.e. have Q1, Q2, C (have Q3, C2)

WILLMORE
Faith, child, I thank God I have ever took care to lead a   250
good, sober, hopeful life, and am of a religion that
teaches me to believe I shall depart in peace.
ANGELLICA
So will the devil! Tell me,
How many poor believing fools thou hast undone?
How many hearts thou hast betrayed to ruin?   255
– Yet these are little mischiefs to the ills
Thou'st taught mine to commit: thou'st taught it love!
WILLMORE
Egad, 'twas shrewdly hurt the while.
ANGELLICA
Love, that has robbed it of its unconcern,
Of all that pride that taught me how to value it.   260
And in its room
A mean submissive passion was conveyed,
That made me humbly bow, which I ne'er did
To anything but Heaven.
Thou, perjured man, didst this, and with thy oaths,   265
Which on thy knees thou didst devoutly make,
Softened my yielding heart – and then, I was a slave.
– Yet still had been content to've worn my chains,
Worn 'em with vanity and joy forever,
Had'st thou not broke those vows that put them on.   270
'Twas then I was undone.

All this while follows him with the pistol to his breast

WILLMORE
Broke my vows! Why, where hast thou lived?
Amongst the gods? For I never heard of mortal man
That has not broke a thousand vows.
ANGELLICA
Oh, impudence!   275
WILLMORE
Angellica! That beauty has been too long tempting
Not to have made a thousand lovers languish,
Who, in the amorous fever, no doubt have sworn
Like me. Did they all die in that faith? Still adoring?
I do not think they did.   280
ANGELLICA
No, faithless man: had I repaid their vows, as I did thine,

250–2 prose ed. (verse Q1)
278 *fever* Q3 (favour Q1, Q2, C, C2)

I would have killed the ingrateful that had abandoned
    me.
WILLMORE
    This old general has quite spoiled thee. Nothing makes
    a woman so vain as being flattered; your old lover ever
    supplies the defects of age with intolerable dotage, vast   285
    charge, and that which you call constancy; and attribu-
    ting all this to your own merits, you domineer, and throw
    your favours in's teeth, upbraiding him still with the
    defects of age, and cuckold him as often as he deceives
    your expectations. But the gay, young, brisk lover, that   290
    brings his equal fires, and can give you dart for dart,
    you'll find will be as nice as you sometimes.
ANGELLICA
    All this thou'st made me know, for which I hate thee.
    Had I remained in innocent security,
    I should have thought all men were born my slaves,   295
    And worn my power like lightning in my eyes,
    To have destroyed at pleasure when offended.
    But when love held the mirror, the undeceiving glass
    Reflected all the weakness of my soul, and made me
       know
    My richest treasure being lost, my honour,   300
    All the remaining spoil could not be worth
    The conqueror's care or value.
    Oh, how I fell like a long-worshipped idol,
    Discovering all the cheat.
    Would not the incense and rich sacrifice   305
    Which blind devotion offered at my altars
    Have fallen to thee?
    Why would'st thou then destroy my fancied power?
WILLMORE
    By Heaven, thou'rt brave, and I admire thee strangely.
    I wish I were that dull, that constant thing   310
    Which thou would'st have, and nature never meant me.
    I must, like cheerful birds, sing in all groves,
    And perch on every bough,
    Billing the next kind she that flies to meet me.
    Yet, after all, could build my nest with thee,   315
    Thither repairing when I'd loved my round,
    And still reserve a tributary flame.
    – To gain your credit, I'll pay you back your charity,

292 *you'll find will* emendation (ms note) in Luttrell Q1 ('you'l will be' Q1; 'he'll be'
    Q2, C, C2; 'will be' Q3)
    nice fastidious

And be obliged for nothing but for love.

Offers her a purse of gold

ANGELLICA

Oh, that thou wert in earnest!   320
So mean a thought of me
Would turn my rage to scorn, and I should pity thee,
And give thee leave to live;
Which, for the public safety of our sex,
And my own private injuries, I dare not do.   325
Prepare –

Follows still as before

I will no more be tempted with replies.
WILLMORE

Sure –
ANGELLICA

Another word will damn thee! I've heard thee talk too
long.   330

*She follows him with the pistol ready to shoot; he retires, still
amazed. Enter* DON ANTONIO, *his arm in a scarf, and lays
hold on the pistol*

ANTONIO

Ha! Angellica!
ANGELLICA

Antonio! What devil brought thee hither?
ANTONIO

Love and curiosity, seeing your coach at door. Let me
disarm you of this unbecoming instrument of death. –
(*Takes away the pistol*) Amongst the number of your   335
slaves, was there not one worthy the honour to have
fought your quarrel? [*To* WILLMORE] – Who are you, sir,
that are so very wretched to merit death from her?
WILLMORE

One, sir, that could have made a better end of an
amorous quarrel without you, than with you.   340
ANTONIO

Sure, 'tis some rival. – Ha! The very man took down her
picture yesterday – the very same that set on me last
night. – Blest opportunity!

Offers to shoot him

335 s.d. Q3 (s.d. follows Antonio's speech Q1, Q2, C, C2)
341–2 *took down her picture* See II.i.101 s.d.

ANGELLICA
  Hold! You're mistaken, sir.
ANTONIO
  By Heaven, the very same!   345
  – Sir, what pretensions have you to this lady?
WILLMORE
  Sir, I do not use to be examined, and am ill at all disputes
  but this –

          Draws: ANTONIO *offers to shoot*

ANGELLICA (*To* WILLMORE)
  Oh, hold! You see he's armed with certain death.
  – And you, Antonio, I command you hold,   350
  By all the passion you've so lately vowed me.

          Enter DON PEDRO, *sees* ANTONIO, *and stays*

PEDRO (*Aside*)
  Ha, Antonio! and Angellica!
ANTONIO
  When I refuse obedience to your will,
  May you destroy me with your mortal hate.
  By all that's holy, I adore you so,   355
  That even my rival, who has charms enough
  To make him fall a victim to my jealousy,
  Shall live; nay, and have leave to love on still.
PEDRO (*Aside*)
  What's this I hear?
ANGELLICA (*pointing to* WILLMORE)
  Ah, thus! 'Twas thus! He talked, and I believed.   360
  – Antonio, yesterday,
  I'd not have sold my interest in his heart
  For all the sword has won and lost in battle.
  [*To* WILLMORE] – But now, to show my utmost of con-
      tempt,
  I give thee life – which if thou would'st preserve,   365
  Live where my eyes may never see thee more,
  Live to undo someone, whose soul may prove
  So bravely constant to revenge my love.
          Goes out. ANTONIO *follows, but* PEDRO *pulls him back*
PEDRO
  Antonio – stay.
ANTONIO
  Don Pedro –   370
PEDRO
  What coward fear was that prevented thee
  From meeting me this morning on the Molo?

ANTONIO
  Meet thee?
PEDRO
  Yes, me. I was the man that dared thee to't.
ANTONIO
  Hast thou so often seen me fight in war,   375
  To find no better cause to excuse my absence?
  I sent my sword and one to do thee right,
  Finding myself incapable to use a sword.
PEDRO
  But 'twas Florinda's quarrel that we fought,
  And you, to show how little you esteemed her,   380
  Sent me your rival, giving him your interest.
  But I have found the cause of this affront,
  And when I meet you fit for the dispute,
  I'll tell you my resentment.
ANTONIO
  I shall be ready, sir, ere long, to do you reason.   *Exit* 385
PEDRO
  If I could find Florinda, now, whilst my anger's high,
  I think I should be kind, and give her to Belvile in
    revenge.
WILLMORE
  Faith, sir, I know not what you would do, but I believe
  the priest within has been so kind.
PEDRO
  How! My sister married?   390
WILLMORE
  I hope by this time she is, and bedded too, or he has not
  my longings about him.
PEDRO
  Dares he do this? Does he not fear my power?
WILLMORE
  Faith, not at all; if you will go in and thank him for the
  favour he has done your sister, so. If not, sir, my power's 395
  greater in this house than yours. I have a damned surly
  crew here that will keep you till the next tide, and then
  clap you on board for prize. My ship lies but a league
  off the Molo, and we shall show your donship a damned
  Tramontana rover's trick.   400

---

378 *incapable* ed. (uncapable Q1)
391 *she* C, C2 (he Q1–3)
400 *Tramontana rover* foreign pirate

Enter BELVILE

BELVILE
This rogue's in some new mischief. – Ha, Pedro
returned!

PEDRO
Colonel Belvile, I hear you have married my sister.

BELVILE
You have heard truth then, sir.

PEDRO
Have I so? Then sir, I wish you joy.   405

BELVILE
How?

PEDRO
By this embrace, I do, and I am glad on't.

BELVILE
Are you in earnest?

PEDRO
By our long friendship and my obligations to thee, I am.
The sudden change, I'll give you reasons for anon.   410
Come, lead me to my sister,
That she may know I now approve her choice.

Exit BELVILE *with* PEDRO. WILLMORE *goes to follow them.*
Enter HELLENA, *as before in boy's clothes, and pulls him*
back

WILLMORE
Ha, my gipsy! – Now a thousand blessings on thee for
this kindness. Egad, child, I was e'en in despair of ever
seeing thee again. My friends are all provided for within,   415
each man his kind woman.

HELLENA
Ha! I thought they had served me some such trick!

WILLMORE
And I was e'en resolved to go abroad, and condemn
myself to my lone cabin, and the thoughts of thee.

HELLENA
And could you have left me behind? Would you have   420
been so ill-natured?

WILLMORE
Why, 'twould have broke my heart, child – but since we
are met again, I defy foul weather to part us.

HELLENA
And would you be a faithful friend now, if a maid should
trust you?   425

still unsure of
his fiedelity

WILLMORE

For a friend, I cannot promise; thou art of a form so
excellent, a face and humour too good for cold, dull
friendship. I am parlously afraid of being in love, child,
and you have not forgot how severely you have used me?

HELLENA

That's all one; such usage you must still look for – to   430
find out all your haunts, to rail at you to all that love
you, till I have made you love only me in your own
defence, because nobody else will love you.

WILLMORE

But hast thou no better quality to recommend thyself
by?   435

HELLENA

Faith, none, captain. Why, 'twill be the greater charity
to take me for thy mistress. I am a lone child, a kind of
orphan lover, and why I should die a maid, and in a
captain's hands, too, I do not understand.

WILLMORE

Egad, I was never clawed away with broadsides from any   440
female before. Thou hast one virtue I adore – good
nature. I hate a coy, demure mistress; she's as troublesome as a colt. I'll break none. No, give me a mad
mistress when mewed, and in flying, one I dare trust
upon the wing that whilst she's kind will come to the   445
lure.

HELLENA

Nay, as kind as you will, good captain, whilst it lasts,
but let's lose no time.

WILLMORE

My time's as precious to me as thine can be; therefore,
dear creature, since we are so well agreed, let's retire to   450
my chamber, and if ever thou wert treated with such
savoury love! Come – my bed's prepared for such a guest
all clean and sweet as thy fair self. I love to steal a dish
and a bottle with a friend, and hate long graces. – Come,
let's retire and fall to.   455

---

433 *love you* Q3 (love Q1, Q2, C, C2)
440 *clawed away* scolded, railed at
  broadsides the simultaneous discharge of artillery from one side of a war-ship
444 *mewed* See III.i.5 note.
  flying, one S, vol. 1, p. 100 (flying on Q1–3, C, C2)
445–6 *come . . . lure* as a bird of prey flies back to the handler for food
455 *fall to* C2 (fall too Q1) See III.i.176 note.

HELLENA

'Tis but getting my consent, and the business is soon
done. Let but old gaffer Hymen and his priest say amen
to't, and I dare lay my mother's daughter by as proper a
fellow as your father's son, without fear or blushing.

WILLMORE

Hold, hold, no bug words, child. Priest and Hymen!   460
Prithee add a hang-man to 'em to make up the consort.
No, no, we'll have no vows but love, child, nor witness
but the lover; the kind deity enjoin naught but love and
enjoy! Hymen and priest wait still upon portion and
jointure; love and beauty have their own ceremonies.   465
Marriage is as certain a bane to love as lending money
is to friendship: I'll neither ask nor give a vow – though
I could be content to turn gipsy, and become a left-
handed bridegroom, to have the pleasure of working
that great miracle of making a maid a mother, if you   470
durst venture. 'Tis upse gipsy that, and if I miss, I'll lose
my labour.

HELLENA

And if you do not lose, what shall I get? A cradle full of
noise and mischief, with a pack of repentance at my
back? Can you teach me to weave incle to pass my time   475
with? 'Tis upse gipsy that, too.

WILLMORE

I can teach thee to weave a true love's knot better.

HELLENA

So can my dog.

WILLMORE

Well, I see we are both upon our guards, and I see there's
no way to conquer good nature, but by yielding. Here –   480
give me thy hand – one kiss and I am thine –

HELLENA

One kiss! How like my page he speaks; I am resolved

---

457 *gaffer* old man
        Hymen god of marriage
460 *bug words* words meant to frighten or threaten
461 *consort* company, partnership
463 *enjoin* ed. (injoin Q1–3; injoins C, C2)
464 *enjoy* (injoy Q1)
        portion marriage portion, dowry
465 *jointure* 1) dowry 2) the joint holding of property by husband and wife 3) the
        agreed provision of lands etc. for the wife, to take effect after the husband's death
468–9 *left-handed bridegroom* i.e. bridegroom of an illegal or fictitious marriage
471 *upse gipsy* in the gipsy fashion
475 *incle* linen thread or yarn from which the tape known as 'incle' was manufactured

you shall have none for asking such a sneaking sum. He
that will be satisfied with one kiss will never die of that
longing; good friend single-kiss, is all your talking come   485
to this? A kiss, a caudle! Farewell captain single-kiss.

Going out, he stays her

WILLMORE
Nay, if we part so, let me die like a bird upon a bough,
at the sheriff's charge. By Heaven, both the Indies shall
not buy thee from me. I adore thy humour and will
marry thee, and we are so of one humour, it must be a   490
bargain. – Give me thy hand (*kisses her hand*) – and now
let the blind ones, love and fortune, do their worst.

HELLENA
Why, God-a-mercy captain!

WILLMORE
But hark'ee – the bargain is now made; but is it not fit
we should know each other's names, that when we have   495
reason to curse one another hereafter, and people ask
me who 'tis I give to the devil, I may at least be able to
tell what family you came of?

HELLENA
Good reason, captain; and where I have cause (as I
doubt not but I shall have plentiful) that I may know at   500
whom to throw my – blessings. I beseech ye your name.

WILLMORE
I am called Robert the Constant.

HELLENA
A very fine name! Pray was it your falconer or butler
that christened you? Do they not use to whistle when
they call you?   505

WILLMORE
I hope you have a better, that a man may name without
crossing himself, you are so merry with mine.

HELLENA
I am called Hellena the Inconstant.

---

486 *caudle* warm drink of thin gruel and wine or ale, given to the sick
487 *let me ... bough* i.e. let me be hanged
492 *blind ... fortune* Both Cupid, god of love, and Fortune were depicted wearing
    blind-folds.
503 *falconer* keeper of hawks
    butler originally, the servant in charge of the wine-cellar. She may be implying
    that he is a predatory man, only steadfast in his attachments to prey (i.e. women),
    and to drink.

Enter PEDRO, BELVILE, FLORINDA,
FREDERICK [*and*] VALERIA

PEDRO
Ha! Hellena!
FLORINDA
Hellena! 510
HELLENA
The very same. Ha, my brother! Now captain, show
your love and courage; stand to your arms and defend
me bravely, or I am lost forever.
PEDRO
What's this I hear? False girl, how came you hither, and
what's your business? Speak. 515

Goes roughly to her

WILLMORE
Hold off, sir; you have leave to parley only.

Puts himself between

HELLENA
I had e'en as good tell it, as you guess it. Faith, brother,
my business is the same with all living creatures of my
age: to love and be beloved, and here's the man.
PEDRO
Perfidious maid, hast thou deceived me, too; deceived 520
thyself and Heaven?
HELLENA
'Tis time enough to make my peace with that,
Be you but kind, let me alone with Heaven.
PEDRO
Belvile, I did not expect this false play from you; was't
not enough you'd gain Florinda (which I pardoned), but 525
your lewd friends, too, must be enriched with the spoils
of a noble family?
BELVILE
Faith, sir, I am as much surprised at this as you can be.
Yet, sir, my friends are gentlemen, and ought to be
esteemed for their misfortunes, since they have the glory 530
to suffer with the best of men and kings; 'tis true, he's a
rover of fortune, yet a prince aboard his little wooden
world.
PEDRO
What's this to the maintenance of a woman of her birth
and quality? 535

525 *you'd gain* Q1, Q2, C, C2 (you gained Q3)

WILLMORE

Faith, sir, I can boast of nothing but a sword which does
me right where'er I come, and has defended a worse
cause than a woman's; and since I loved her before I
either knew her birth or name, I must pursue my resolution, and marry her.   540

PEDRO [*to* HELLENA]

And is all your holy intent of becoming a nun, debauched
into a desire of man?

HELLENA

Why, I have considered the matter, brother, and find the
two hundred thousand crowns my uncle left me (and
you cannot keep from me) will be better laid out in love   545
than in religion, and turn to as good an account. – Let
most voices carry it: for Heaven or the captain?

ALL (*cry*)

A captain! A captain!

HELLENA

Look ye, sir, 'tis a clear case.

PEDRO

Oh, I am mad! (*Aside*) – If I refuse, my life's in danger. –   550
Come, there's one motive induces me. Take her. I shall
now be free from fears of her honour; guard it you now,
if you can. I have been a slave to't long enough.

Gives her to [WILLMORE]

WILLMORE

Faith, sir, I am of a nation that are of opinion a woman's
honour is not worth guarding when she has a mind to   555
part with it.

HELLENA

Well said, captain.

PEDRO (*To* VALERIA)

This was your plot, mistress, but I hope you have married
one that will revenge my quarrel to you.

VALERIA

There's no altering destiny, sir.   560

PEDRO

Sooner than a woman's will; therefore I forgive you all –
and wish you may get my father's pardon as easily; which
I fear.

544 *two* Q3 (three Q1, Q2, C, C2) See IV.ii.192–3.

Enter BLUNT, *dressed in a Spanish habit, looking
very ridiculously, his* MAN *adjusting his band*

MAN
    'Tis very well, sir –
BLUNT
    Well, sir! 'Adsheartlikins, I tell you 'tis damnable ill, sir.   565
    A Spanish habit! Good Lord! Could the devil and my
    tailor devise no other punishment for me but the mode
    of a nation I abominate?
BELVILE
    What's the matter, Ned?
BLUNT
    Pray view me round, and judge –   570

Turns round

BELVILE
    I must confess thou art a kind of an odd figure.
BLUNT
    In a Spanish habit with a vengeance! I had rather be in
    the Inquisition for Judaism than in this doublet and
    breeches; a pillory were an easy collar to this three
    handfuls high; and these shoes, too, are worse than the   575
    stocks, with the sole an inch shorter than my foot. In
    fine, gentlemen, methinks I look altogether like a bag of
    bays stuffed full of fool's flesh.
BELVILE
    Methinks 'tis well, and makes thee look e'en cavalier.
    Come, sir, settle your face and salute our friends. Lady –   580
BLUNT (*To* HELLENA)
    Ha! Say'st thou so, my little rover? Lady – if you be
    one – give me leave to kiss your hand, and tell you,
    'adsheartlikins, for all I look so, I am your humble
    servant. – A pox of my Spanish habit!

563 s.d. 1 *habit* See I.i.210 note.
    s.d. 2 *band* probably his neck band or collar. See ll. 474–5.
573 *Inquisition for Judaism* Punishments were especially severe in Spain, where the
    Inquisition had been reorganised by the state and directed against Jews and
    Moors.
    doublet close-fitting upper garment
574 *pillory* a wooden frame through which the head and hands of an offender were
    thrust and exposed to public insult
576 *stocks* wooden boards locked around an offender's feet with the same purpose as
    the pillory
577–8 *bag of bays* a porous bag of bay leaves and spices used in cooking
579 *e'en* even

WILLMORE

Hark, what's this?   585

Music is heard to play
Enter BOY

BOY

Sir, as the custom is, the gay people in masquerade, who make every man's house their own, are coming up.

Enter several men and women in masking habits,
with music; they put themselves in order and dance

BLUNT

'Adsheartlikins, would 'twere lawful to pull off their false faces, that I might see if my doxy were not amongst 'em.

BELVILE (*To the maskers*)

Ladies and gentlemen, since you are come so *à propos*,   590
you must take a small collation with us.

WILLMORE (*To* HELLENA)

Whilst we'll to the good man within, who stays to give us a cast of his office. Have you no trembling at the near approach?

HELLENA

No more than you have in an engagement or a tempest.   595

WILLMORE

Egad, thou'rt a brave girl, and I admire thy love and courage.

Lead on, no other dangers they can dread,
Who venture in the storms o'th' marriage bed.

Exeunt

completely suited?

590 s.d. *maskers* Q3, C, C2 (masqueros Q1, Q2)
      à propos opportunely
591 *collation* See III.i.171 note.
593 *cast . . . office* i.e. a taste of his office – and, therefore, marriage
595 *engagement* i.e. in fighting or in battle

EPILOGUE

The banished cavaliers! A roving blade!
A popish carnival! A masquerade!
The devil's in't if this will please the nation
In these our blessed times of reformation,
When conventickling is so much in fashion.   5
And yet –
That mutinous tribe less factions do beget,
Than your continual differing in wit.
Your judgement's, as your passion's, a disease:
Nor muse nor miss your appetite can please;   10
You're grown as nice as queasy consciences,
Whose each convulsion, when the spirit moves,
Damns everything that maggot disapproves.
    With canting rule you would the stage refine,
And to dull method all our sense confine.   15
With th' insolence of commonwealths you rule,
Where each gay fop and politic grave fool
On monarch wit impose, without control.
As for the last, who seldom sees a play,
Unless it be the old Blackfriars way;   20
Shaking his empty noddle o'er bamboo,
He cries, 'Good faith, these plays will never do!
Ah, sir, in my young days, what lofty wit,
What high-strained scenes of fighting there were writ.
These are slight airy toys. But tell me, pray,   25
What has the House of Commons done today?'
Then shows his politics, to let you see
Of state affairs he'll judge as notably
As he can do of wit and poetry.
The younger sparks, who hither do resort,   30
Cry,
'Pox o' your genteel things! Give us more sport!

   1 *The banished cavaliers* the play's sub-title
      blade gallant, free and easy fellow
   5 *conventickling* meeting as a non-conformist religious assembly
   7 *That ... tribe* the dissenters
  13 *maggot* person of perverse fancies
  14 *canting* hypocritical
  20 *Blackfriars* one of the earliest indoor theatres
  21 *o'er bamboo* over a walking stick
  32 *genteel* Q3 (gentile Q1, Q2; gentle C, C2)

Damn me, I'm sure 'twill never please the court.'
  Such fops are never pleased, unless the play
Be stuffed with fools as brisk and dull as they.   35
Such might the half-crown spare, and in a glass
At home behold a more accomplished ass,
Where they may set their cravats, wigs, and faces,
And practise all their buffoon'ry grimaces:
See how this – huff becomes, – this damny, – stare,   40
Which they at home may act because they dare,
But must with prudent caution do elsewhere.
Oh that our Nokes, or Tony Lee, could show
A fop but half so much to th' life as you.

40 *damny* damn me! (expletive)
43 *Nokes ... Lee* famous contemporary comedians

POSTSCRIPT

This play had been sooner in print, but for a report about
the town (made by some either very malicious or very
ignorant) that 'twas *Thomaso* altered; which made the booksellers fear some trouble from the proprietor of that admirable play, which indeed has wit enough to stock a poet, and   5
is not to be pieced or mended by any but the excellent
author himself. That I have stolen some hints from it, may
be a proof that I valued it more than to pretend to alter it.
Had I had the dexterity of some poets, who are not more
expert in stealing than in the art of concealing, and who   10
even that way outdo the Spartan boys, I might have appro-
priated all to myself; but I, vainly proud of my judgement,
hang out the sign of Angellica (the only stolen object) to
give notice where a great part of the wit dwelt; though if
the play of *The Novella* were as well worth remembering as   15
Thomaso, they might (bating the name) have as well said I
took it from thence. I will only say the plot and business (not
to boast on't) is my own; as for the words and characters, I
leave the reader to judge and compare 'em with *Thomaso*,
to whom I recommend the great entertainment of reading   20
it. Though had this succeeded ill, I should have had no
need of imploring that justice from the critics, who are
naturally so kind to any that pretend to usurp their
dominion, especially of our sex, they would doubtless have
given me the whole honour on't. Therefore I will only say   25
in English what the famous Virgil does in Latin: I make
verses, and others have the fame.

FINIS

---

3 *Thomaso Thomaso, or, The Wanderer*: a closet drama by Thomas Killigrew, written
  in 1654
8 *it.* ed. (it, Q1)
11 *boys,* ed. (boys. Q1)
15 *The Novella* Richard Brome's comedy of intrigue (1632)
24 *especially . . . sex* omitted in Q1 first issue and some copies of the second issue

NEW MERMAIDS

The Alchemist
All for Love
Arden of Faversham
Bartholmew Fair
The Beaux' Stratagem
The Changeling
A Chaste Maid in Cheapside
The Country Wife
The Critic
Dr Faustus
The Duchess of Malfi
The Dutch Courtesan
Eastward Ho!
Edward the Second
Epicoene or The Silent Woman
Every Man In His Humour
Gammer Gurton's Needle
An Ideal Husband
The Importance of Being Earnest
The Jew of Malta
The Knight of the Burning Pestle
Lady Windermere's Fan
Love for Love
The Malcontent
The Man of Mode
Marriage A-la-Mode
A New Way to Pay Old Debts

The Old Wife's Tale
The Playboy of the Western World
The Provoked Wife
The Recruiting Officer
The Relapse
The Revenger's Tragedy
The Rivals
The Roaring Girl
The Rover
The School for Scandal
She Stoops to Conquer
The Shoemaker's Holiday
The Spanish Tragedy
Tamburlaine
Three Late Medieval Morality Plays
    Mankind
    Everyman
    Mundus et Infans
'Tis Pity She's a Whore
Volpone
The Way of the World
The White Devil
The Witch
The Witch of Edmonton
A Woman Killed with Kindness
A Woman of No Importance
Women Beware Women

NEW MERMAIDS

General editor: Brian Gibbons
Professor of English Literature, University of Münster

The interior of a Restoration theatre
drawn by C. Walter Hodges